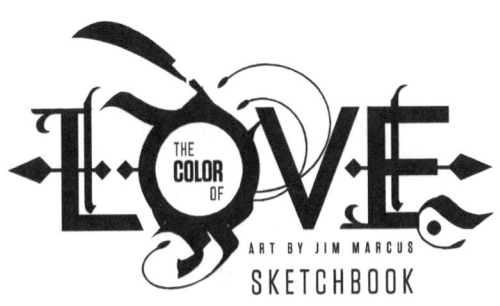

THE COLOR OF LOVE

ART BY JIM MARCUS

SKETCHBOOK

12 3 9 8 4
PULSEBLACK

The Color of Love Sketchbook

by Jim Marcus

June 2024

This book is set in Lato Regular 9/13
Titles in Lato Heavy 16/20

Cover:
Serenaded

by Jim Marcus 2023

ISBN 979-8-9917282-3-2

For Jon Schy, Ryan Stewart, Jan Valle, Jimx, Nicole Ross, and everyone else who has been a part of making real inspiration in the world.

Introduction

....

In Black and White
By Jim Marcus

When I was younger, I developed a passion for black and white design work.

The prioritization of shape over shading and color was fascinating to me. Eventually, it drew me into typography and glyph design, even to being part of the launch of T-26, one of the early leaders in on-the-edge typography in the Early 90s.

My drawings were always in black and white, pencils, markers, even crayons were always white on black or black on white. I immersed myself in logo design, core branding, creating shapes that could communicate a brand even without color, even without shading. I had a fax machine and it was rare I designed anything that didn't pass through it at least once. I had a black and white copier long past the point where most people had color ones.

I'd love to be able to say that this was all willful and intentional and I was just a fun, quirky kid. But the truth was that I had to spend some time, usually every month, colorblind.

My doctor had told me it's called idiopathic achromatopsia. Which is not so much a diagnosis as it is a description. It basically means, "You can't see colors, we don't know why," and, for me, it was due to migraines.

I experienced migraines a couple of times a month. Every third one or so would be so intense that I would sort of feel a "pop" and then my color vision woudl disappear for a day or so. The headache woudl lessen a bit, thouughm, so that was the payoff.

I had heard that other people experienced simiilar things. The brain is like, "Way too much going on," and pulls back on something. I have met people who lose part of their hearing for a day or so, people who lose peripheral vision, even one person who experiences exactly the same thing.

So when I couldn't see color, I couldn't do much actual art of design. Music wasn't easy because my head hurt. Writing was hard because it wouldn't be easy to focus.

But drawing silly little sketches or shapes in black and white seemed to be something I could do. In fact, I could do it sitting in a darkened room with a bright white piece of printer paper,

I would draw shapes for my 'shape library' that I would refer to again and again for logos. And i woudl draw little sketches t amuse myself. Nobody was ever meant to see them. So most of the were either aliens, monsters, or naked people. This is the trifecta, i think, for the ID looking to draw a picture. Scary or Sexy.

Earlier this year, I decided to take a bunch of these drawings, ones I've made over the last 20 years, and blow them up, colorize them, etc. Some I just repainted. Some I put in the projector and drew them again large,. Some I even made stencils or giant stickers of and painted on them.

I called the show, "The Color of Love" and chose about eighty of my sexy drawings. My friends were kind abouut it considering how many genitalia were present.

In this sketchbook, youu will find some drawigs from that, some made after, and some that didn't make it to a painting. I hope it's something you can enjoy, even if your world is color today.

Acrylic Marker Drawings

These were generally drawn on a single sheet of paper using varying weight micro line black acrylic pens and then photographed.

In a lot of cases, I played with rubbing wet ink areas over textures to try to get some fun repeating patterns. You can often tell when this DIDN'T work and I just blacked out the entire area.

I've been exploring what a lot of outisder artists suggest when drawing, which is to sort of turn off my thinking brain and make backgrounds, just expressive washes of line and ink.

Because these are all black and white, all expression like that has to come from shapes. I invented a language for the work that was in my last show and making up words, letterforms, etc. has been one of the most rewarding parts of drawing I do tend to NOT create one to one letterforms, more relying on phonentic work.

Kateera, the letter group here, is an example. It was not the final one used.

Kateera ( )

CONSONANTS

PIG	BED	TIME	DO	CHURCH	JUDGE
KILO	GO	FIVE	VERY	THINK	THE
SIX	ZOO	SHORT	CASUAL	MILK	NO
SING	HELLO	YES	READ	WINDOW	LIVE

VOWELS

SEE	SIT	BOOK	HERE	DAY
TOO	MEN	AMERICA	TOUR	BOY
WORD	SORT	CAT	GO	WEAR
BUT	PART	NOT	MY	HOW

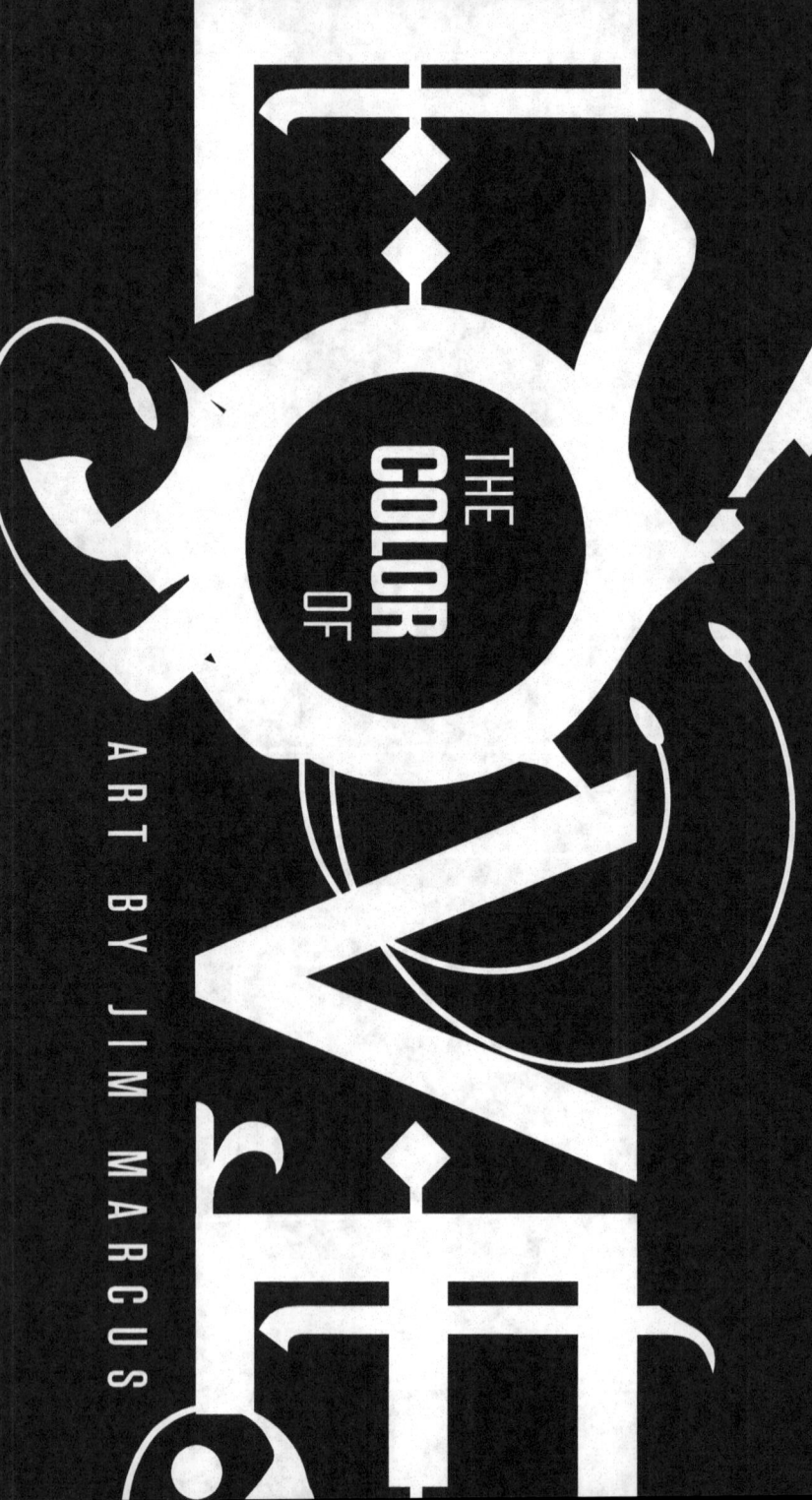

THE
COLOR
OF

ART BY JIM MARCUS

The Show Logo

My goal was to do something that felt modern while, at the same time, did not feel like a part of any time period distinctly.

I've always loved exploring blackletter typography as a means to create something unique but legible and relatable. In a lot of ways, blackletter is the fetishized form of letters.

Often throughout history, when a product or idea is fetishized, when people are passionate about it, its typogrsphic representation is overly elaborate and hyperdesigned. This is an intentional act of love, of wanting to LIVE in that world.

You see this trend on car logos and designs, extraordinarily overdesigned to a purpose. You see it on alcohol bottles. And in blackletter, a type movement from a specific point in history, you saw that same idealization, overdesign, needless flourish. This was a period in history when the actual written word was fetishized.

When you look through some of what is here, you may feel that same sort of passion, I hope, in the refusal to minimize design.

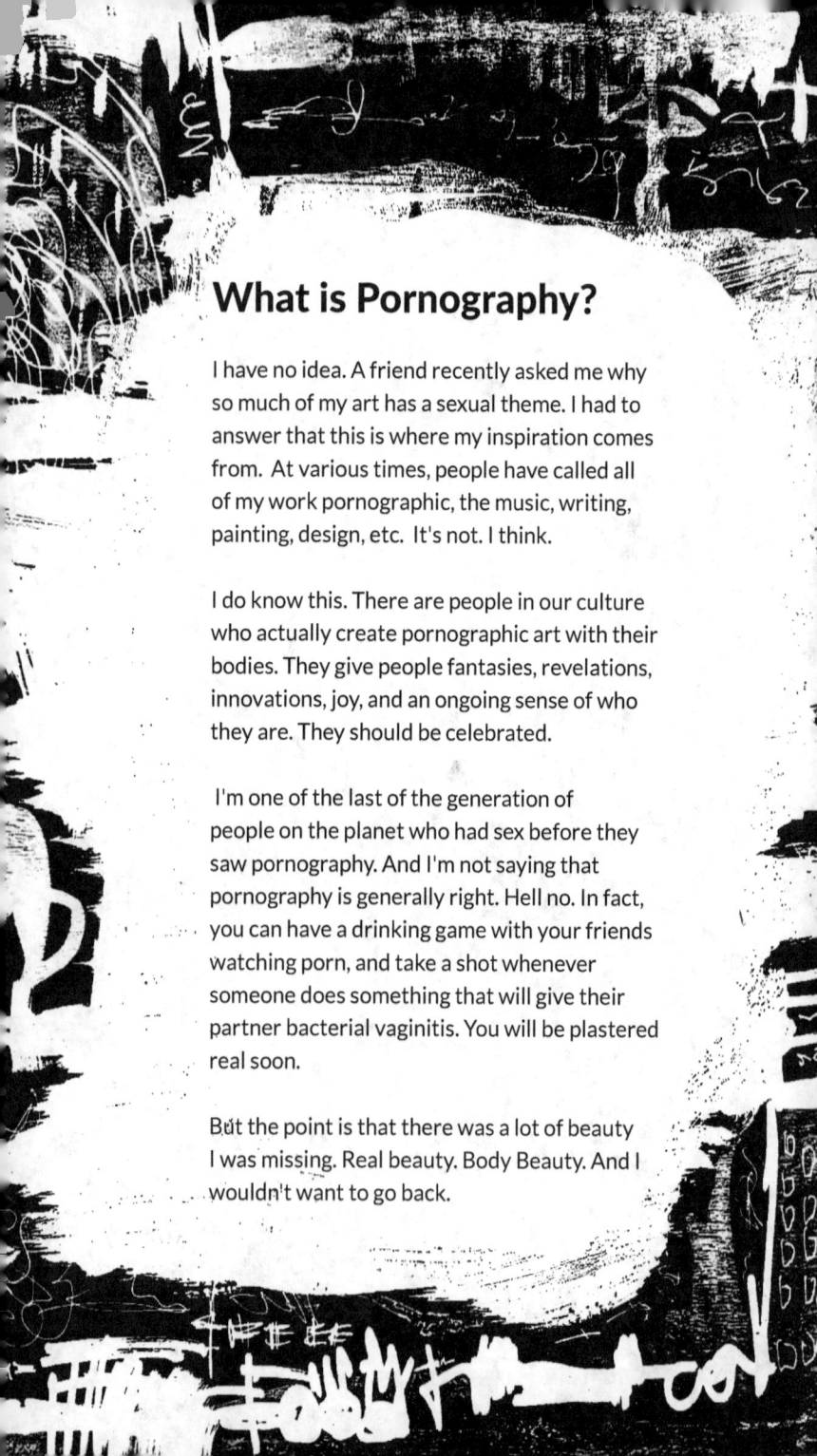

What is Pornography?

I have no idea. A friend recently asked me why so much of my art has a sexual theme. I had to answer that this is where my inspiration comes from. At various times, people have called all of my work pornographic, the music, writing, painting, design, etc. It's not. I think.

I do know this. There are people in our culture who actually create pornographic art with their bodies. They give people fantasies, revelations, innovations, joy, and an ongoing sense of who they are. They should be celebrated.

I'm one of the last of the generation of people on the planet who had sex before they saw pornography. And I'm not saying that pornography is generally right. Hell no. In fact, you can have a drinking game with your friends watching porn, and take a shot whenever someone does something that will give their partner bacterial vaginitis. You will be plastered real soon.

But the point is that there was a lot of beauty I was missing. Real beauty. Body Beauty. And I wouldn't want to go back.

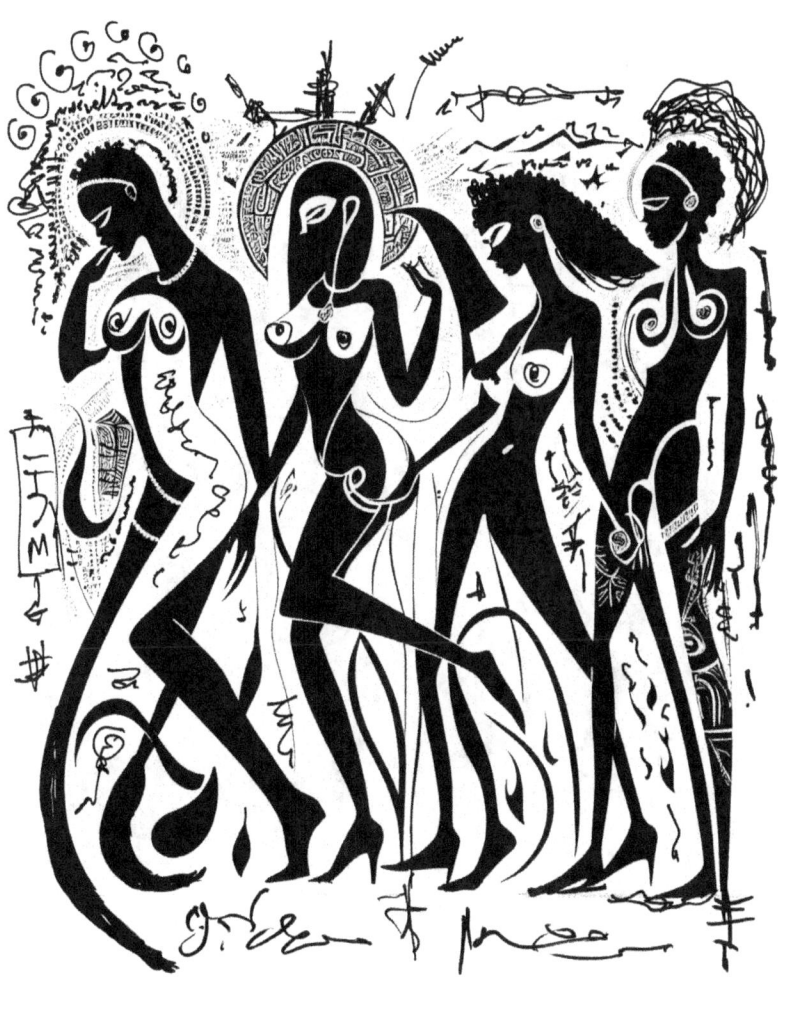

A Perfectly Innocent Tuesday. Acrylic Ink Marker on paper. 2024

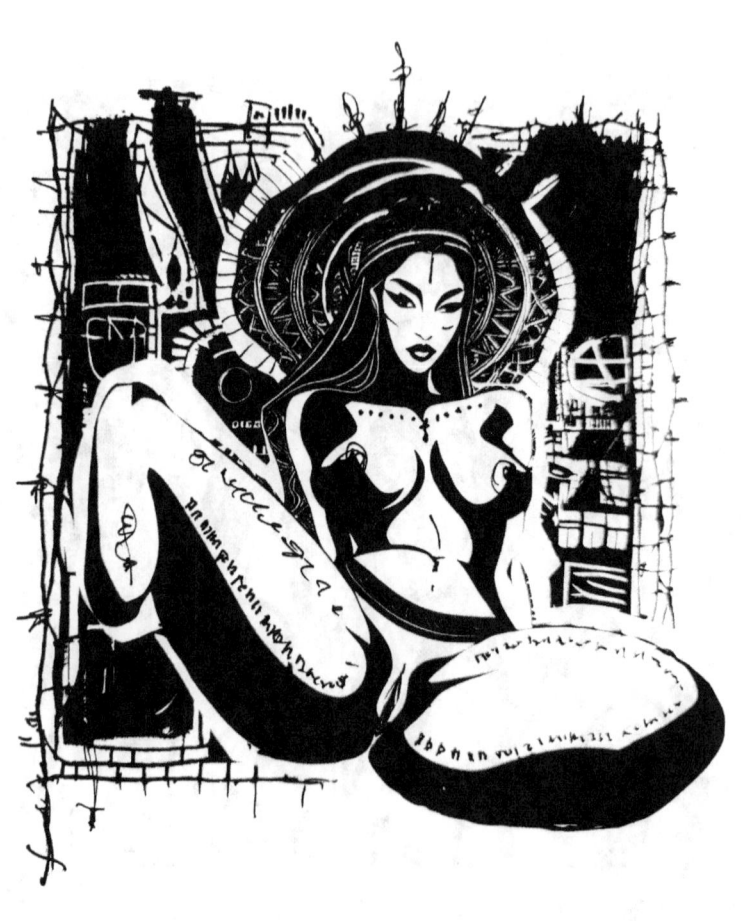

Raven. Acrylic Ink Marker on paper. 2024

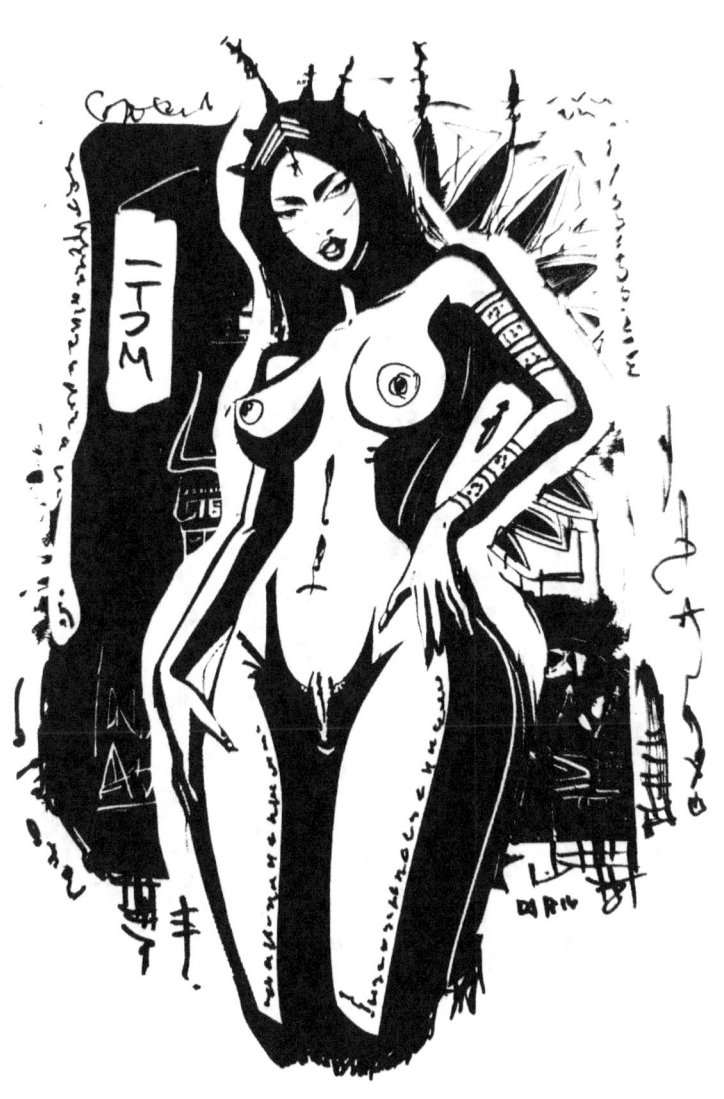

Stand Up. Acrylic Ink Marker on paper. 2024

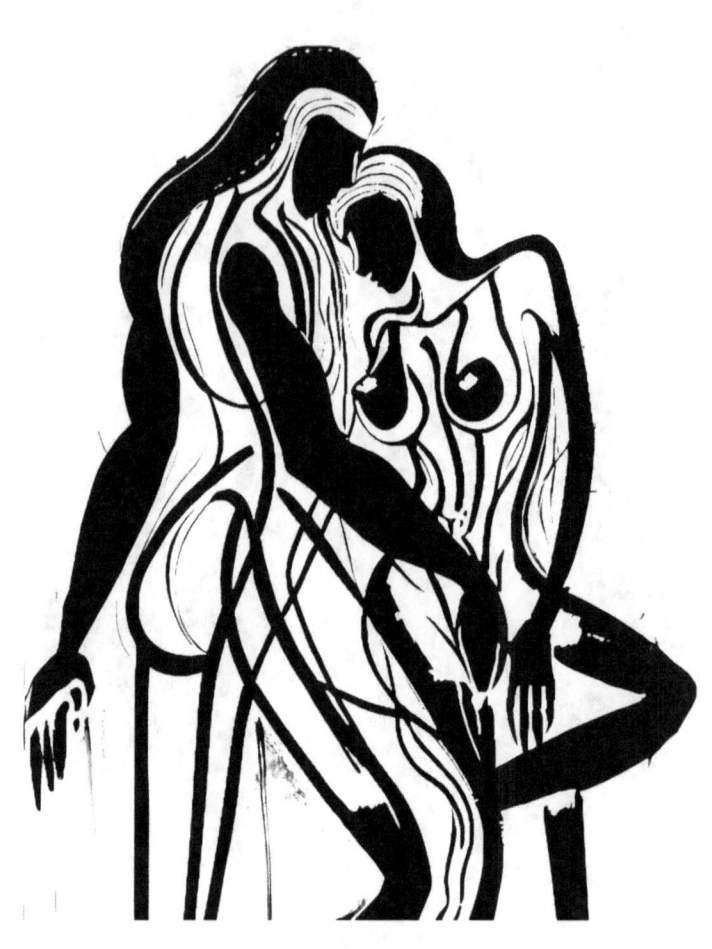

SlowDance Acrylic Ink Marker on paper. 2024

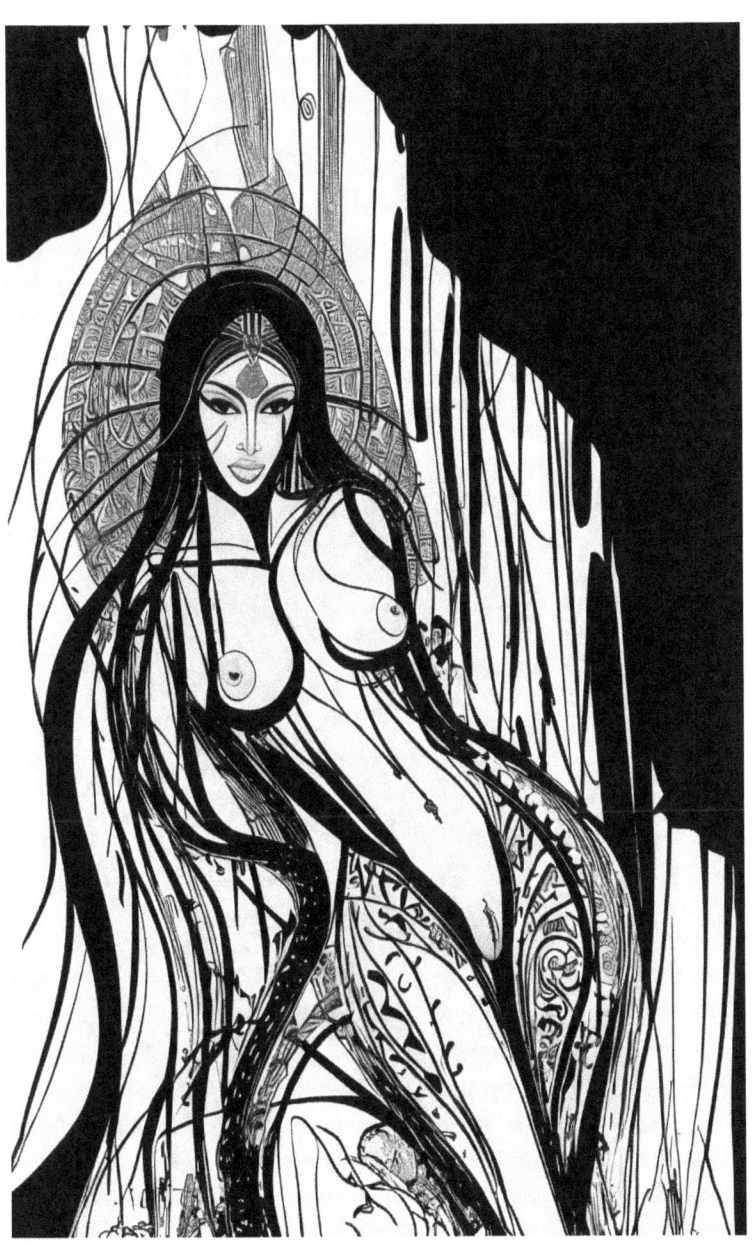

God of Motion. Acrylic Ink Marker on paper. 2024

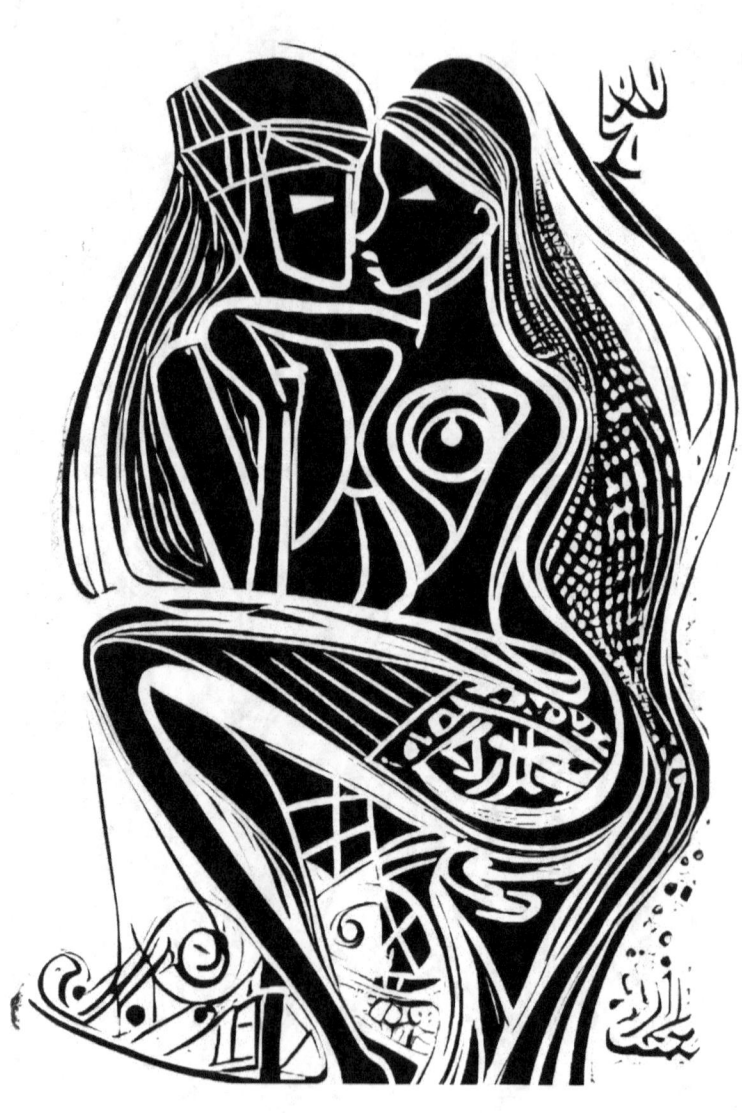

Entwined. Acrylic Ink Marker on paper. 2024

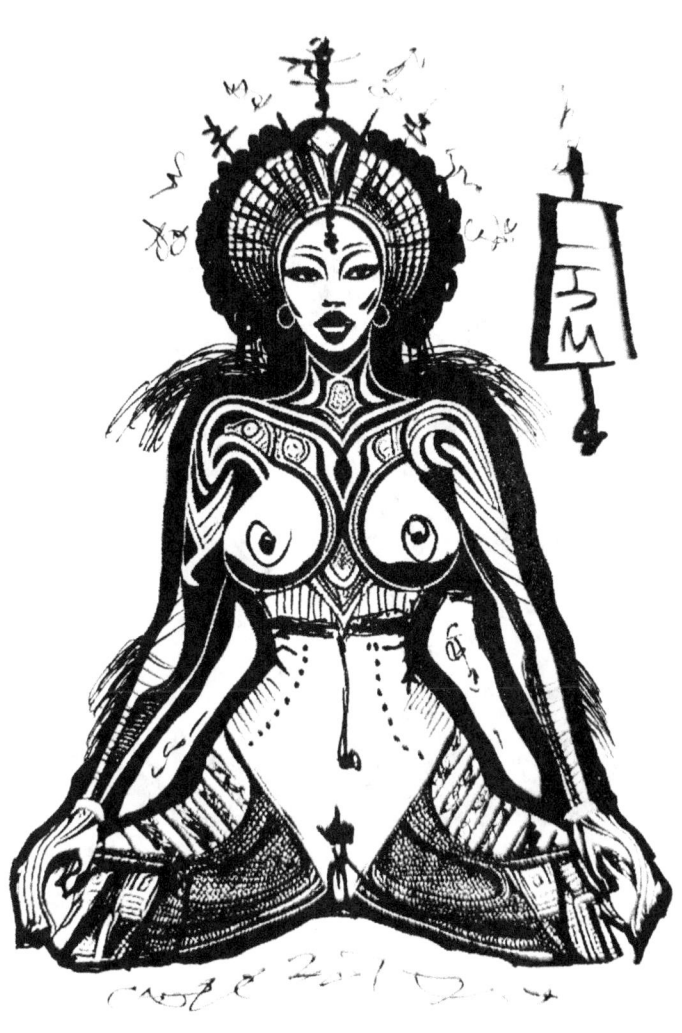

Aria. Acrylic Ink Marker on paper. 2024

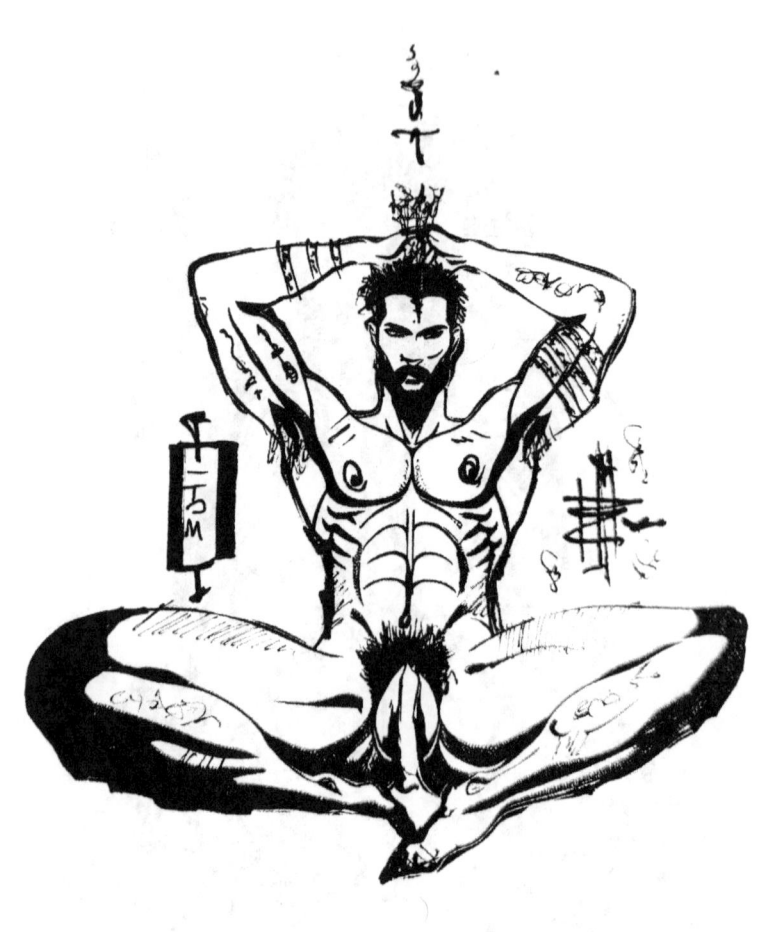

Abe. Acrylic Ink Marker on paper. 2024

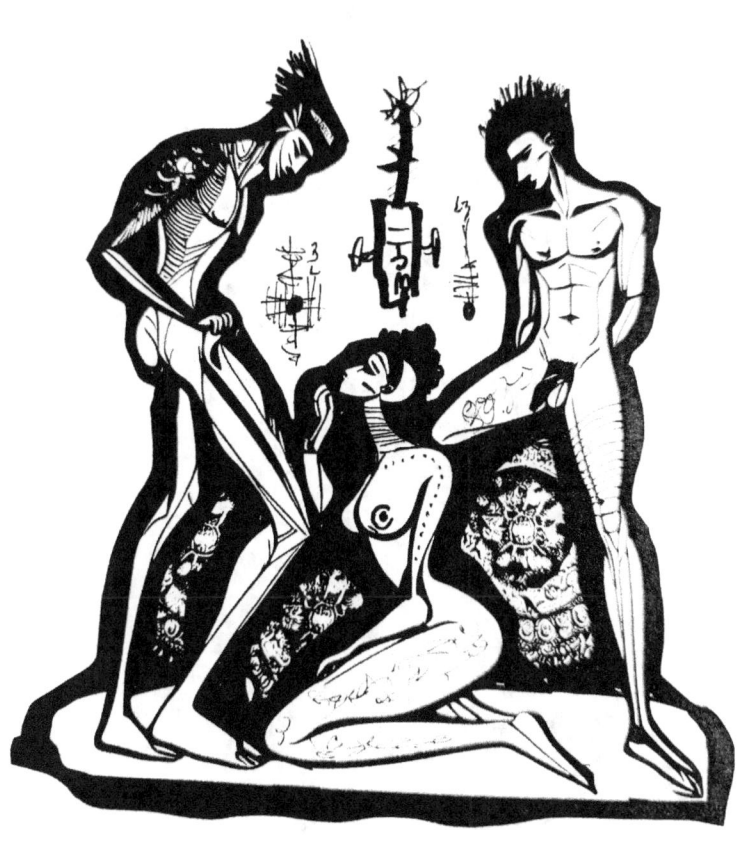

The Circle. Acrylic Ink Marker on paper. 2024

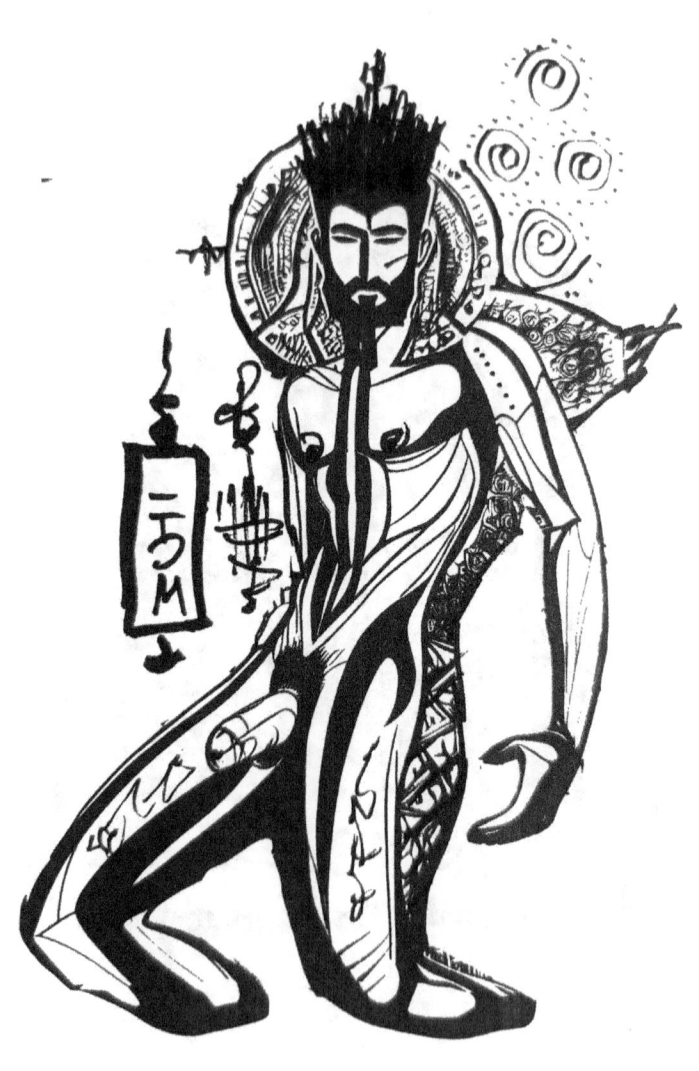

Layne. Acrylic Ink Marker on paper. 2024

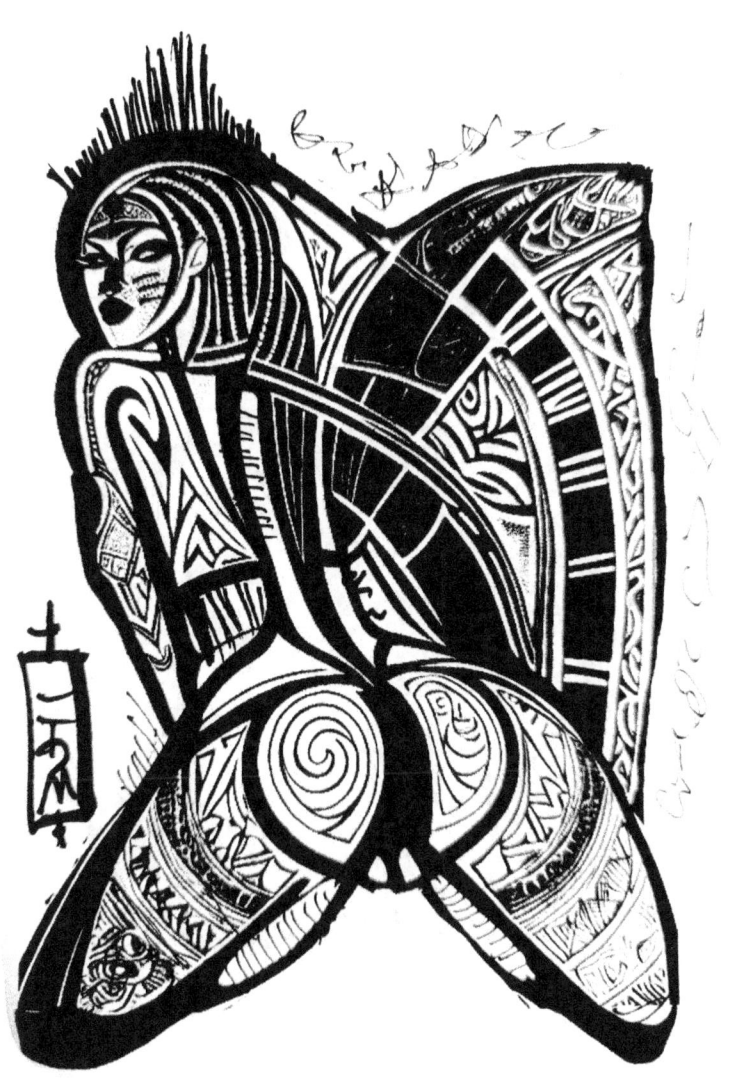

Cat Girl. Acrylic Ink Marker on paper. 2024

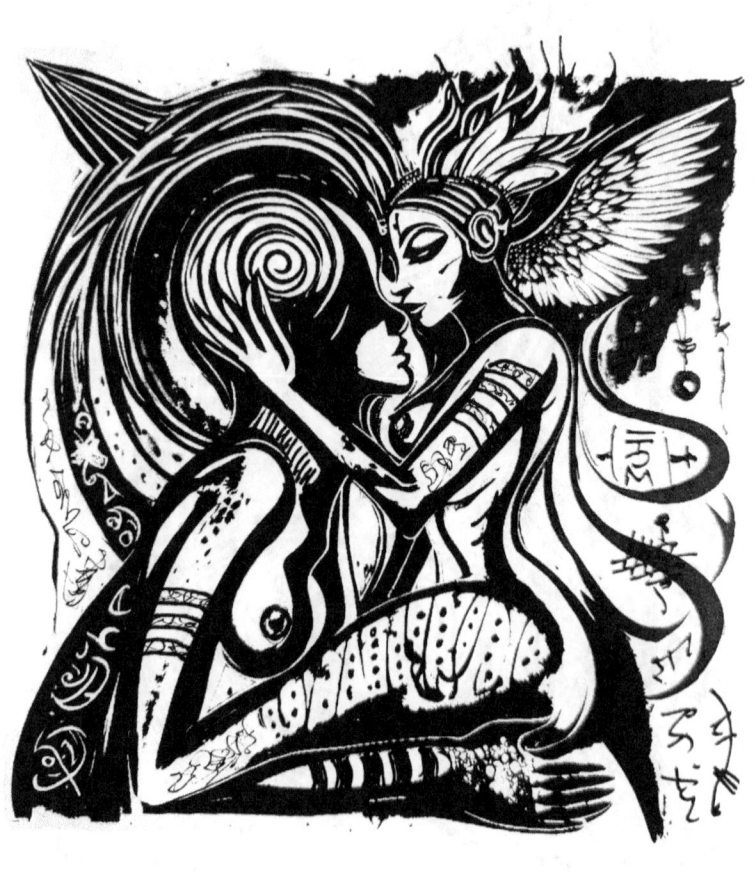

Metatron. Acrylic Ink Marker on paper. 2024

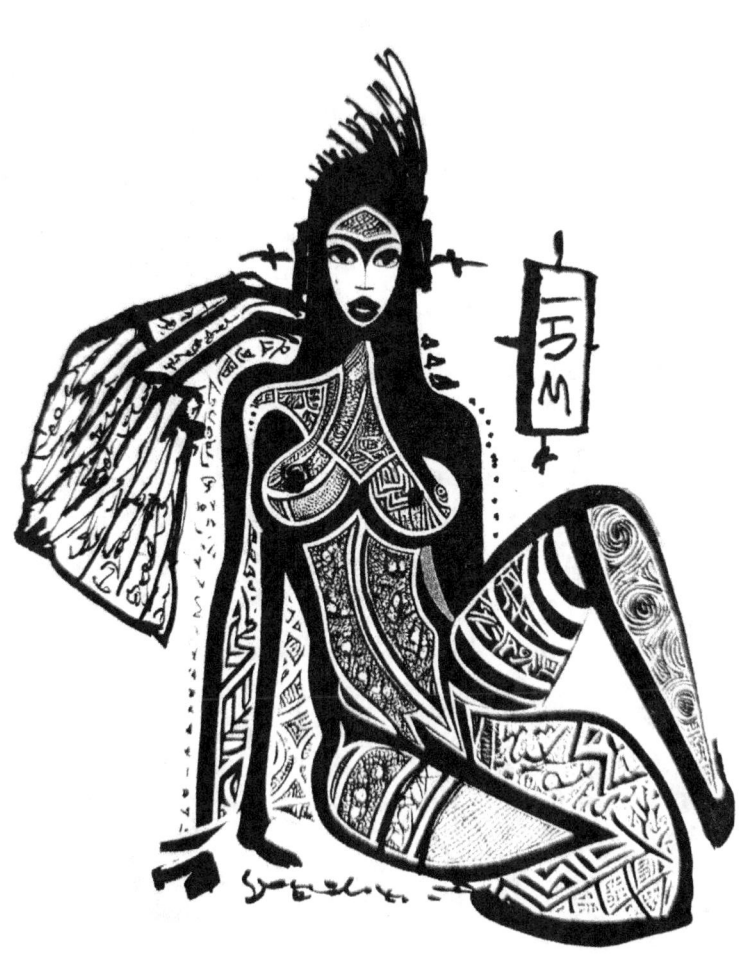

Lila. Acrylic Ink Marker on paper. 2024

About Polyamory

I've been polyamorous my adult life and I know it's not something that is always easy to communicate to people. I don't think that loving someone or being intimate with someone needs to stop you from loving someone else. Love, in my experience, is effulgent, not selfish.

I've tried, thoroughout my art, to find ways to showcase poly in a normative and healthy way, but, in all honesty it always ends up looking and feeling seedy and overly sexualized to people, no matter what you do.

So, I stopped caring so much. If most of the characters I paint or draw look like they are in love, joyful, passionate, that's fine, I realized, in my work that I have used a lot of symbolism without even trying. Halos and elaborate designs around people's heads suggest they are in love. Wings tend to suggest freedom, netting tends to indicate safety.

I know that a lot of symbolism is universal. It is meant to be connective between people, regardless of where they come from. I hope that is true. I hope to connect.

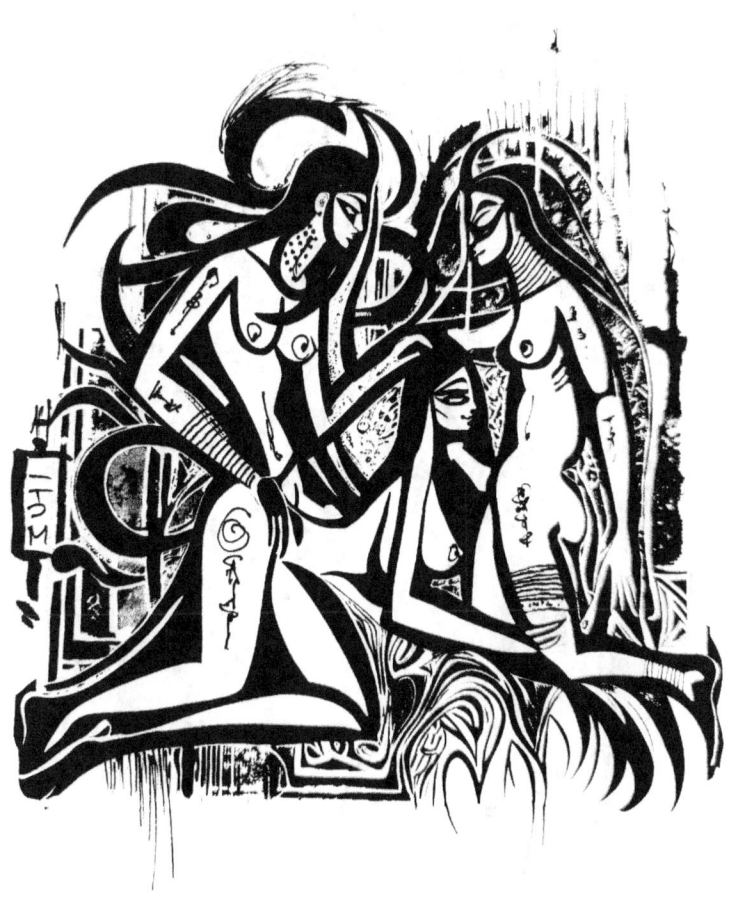

The loop. Acrylic Ink Marker on paper. 2024

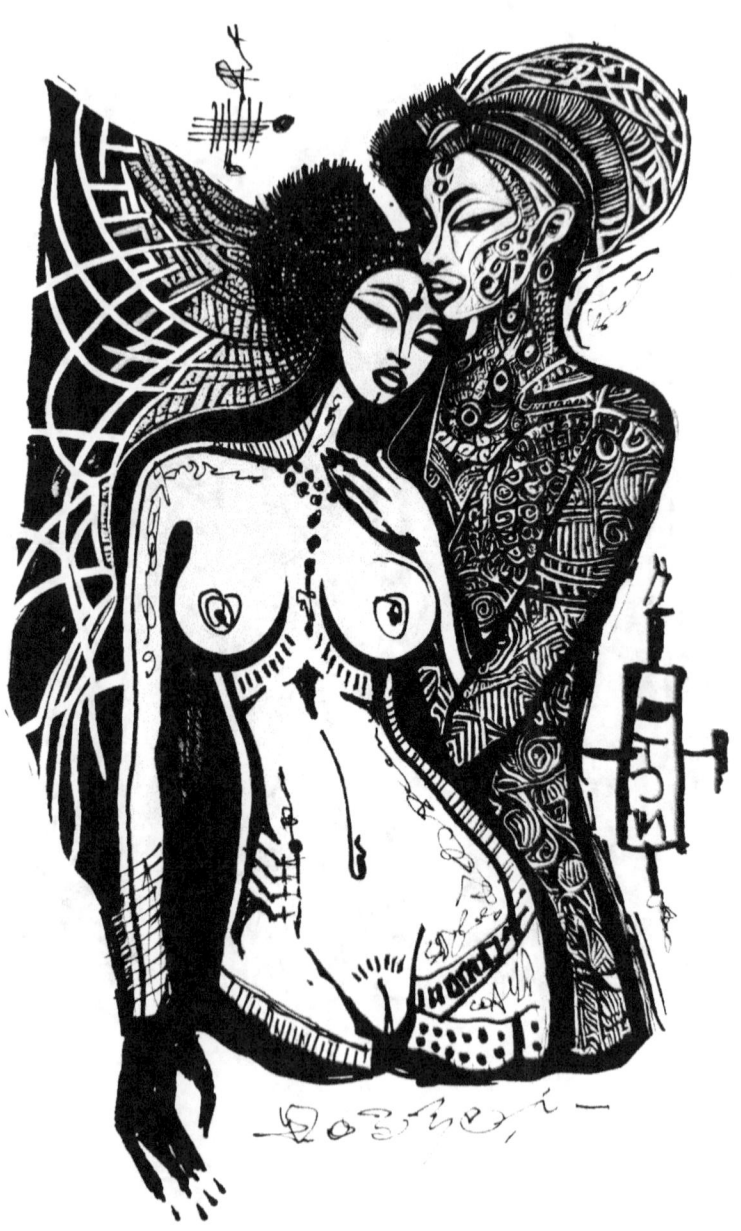

The Cloak. Acrylic Ink Marker on paper. 2024

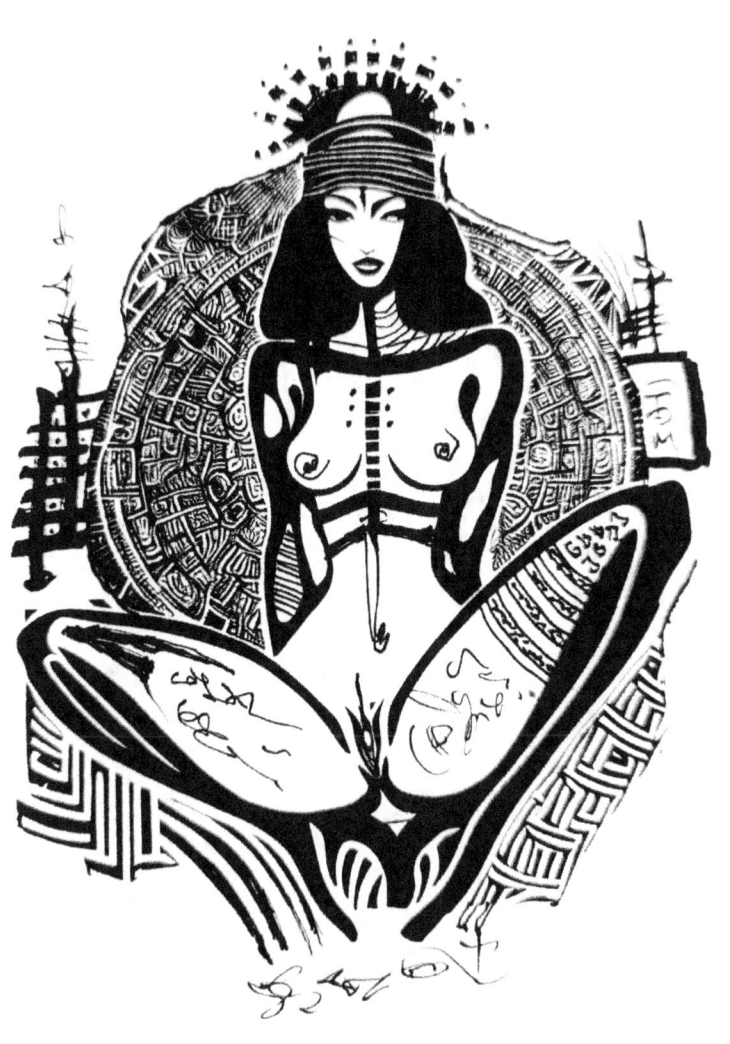

Aburrada. Acrylic Ink Marker on paper. 2024

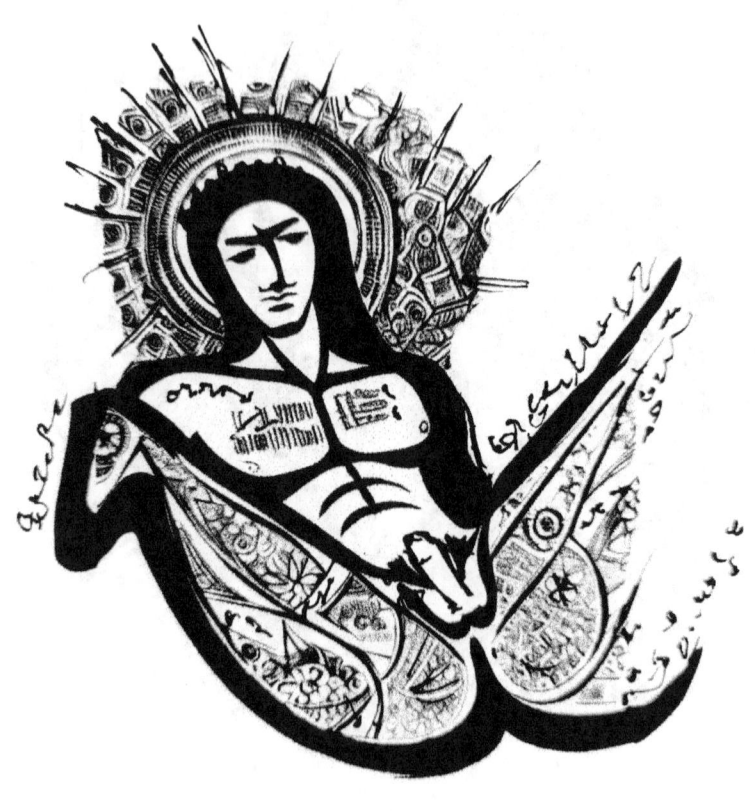

Rialto. Acrylic Ink Marker on paper. 2024

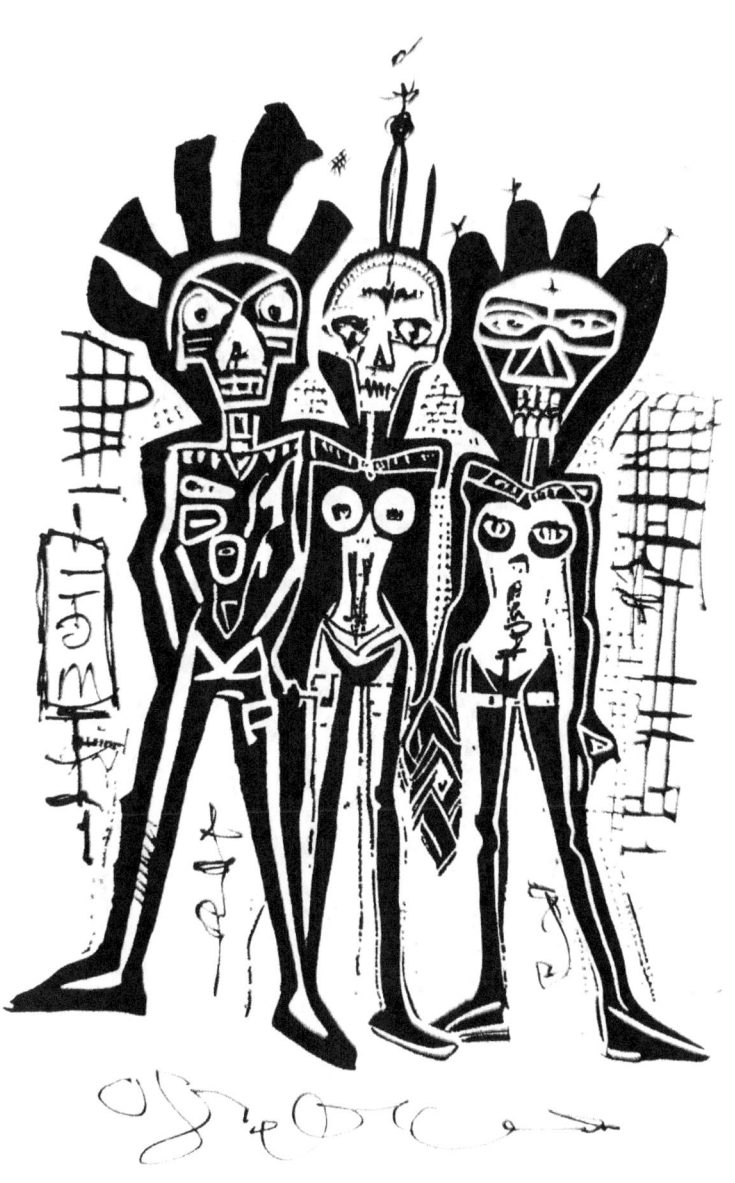

Sex Punx. Acrylic Ink Marker on paper. 2024

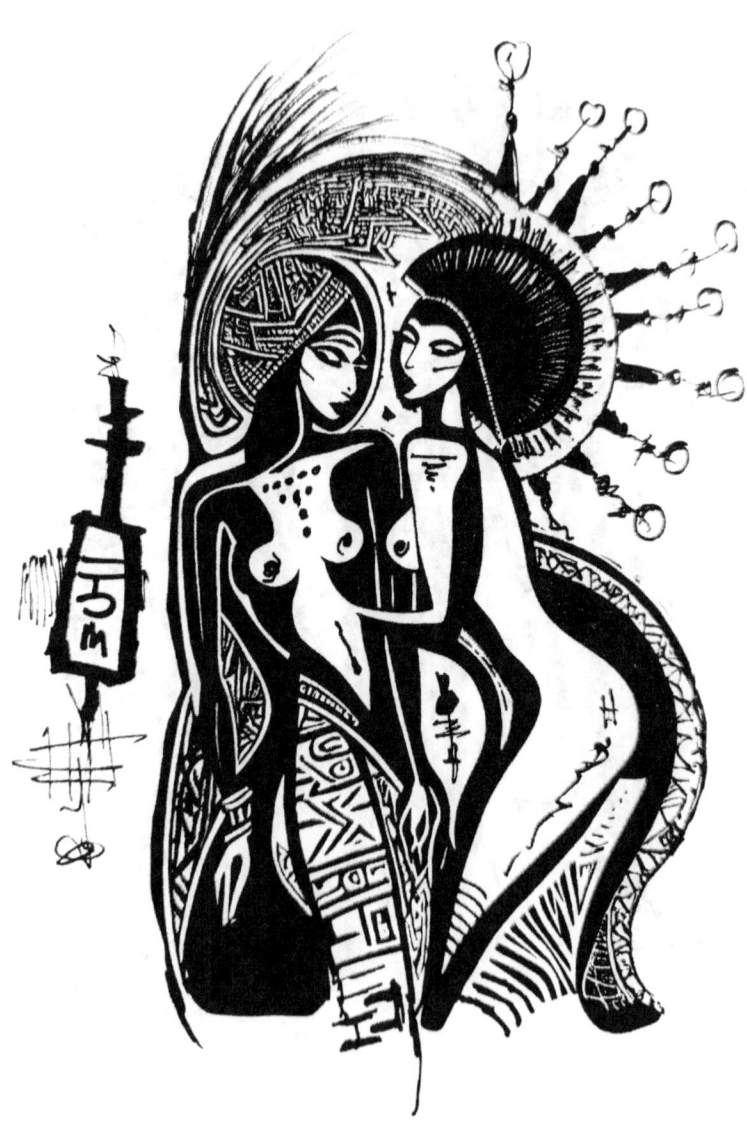

The night vision. Acrylic Ink Marker on paper. 2024

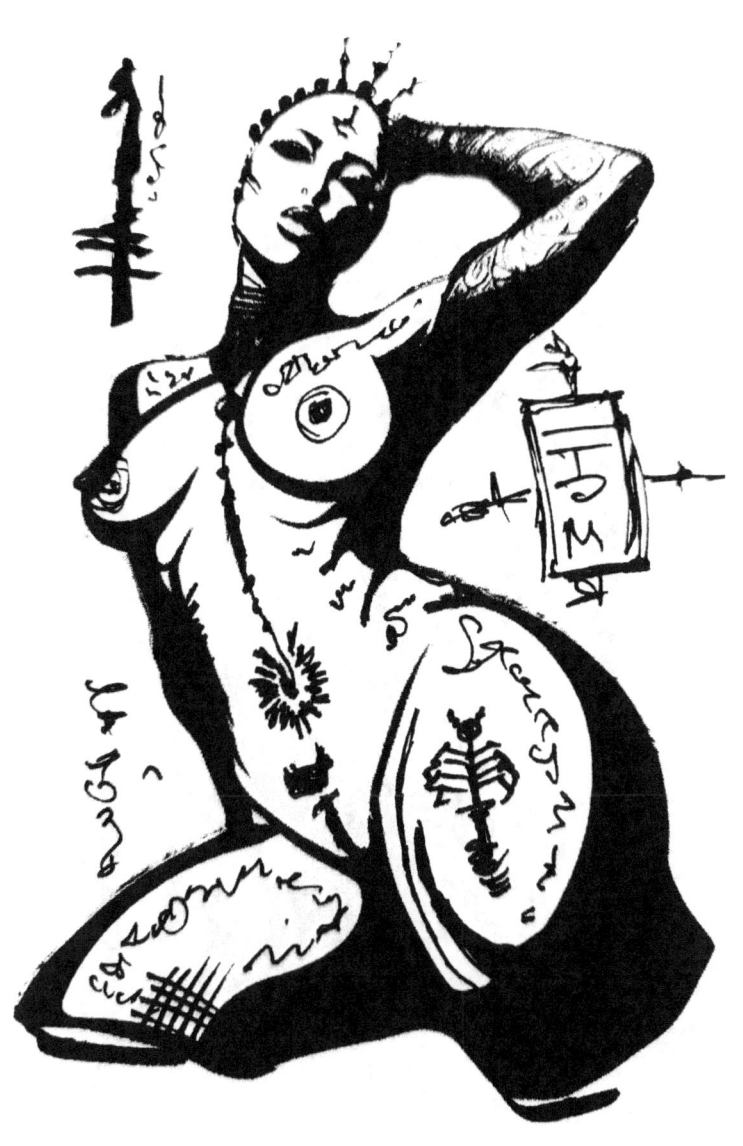

GeeBee. Acrylic Ink Marker on paper. 2024

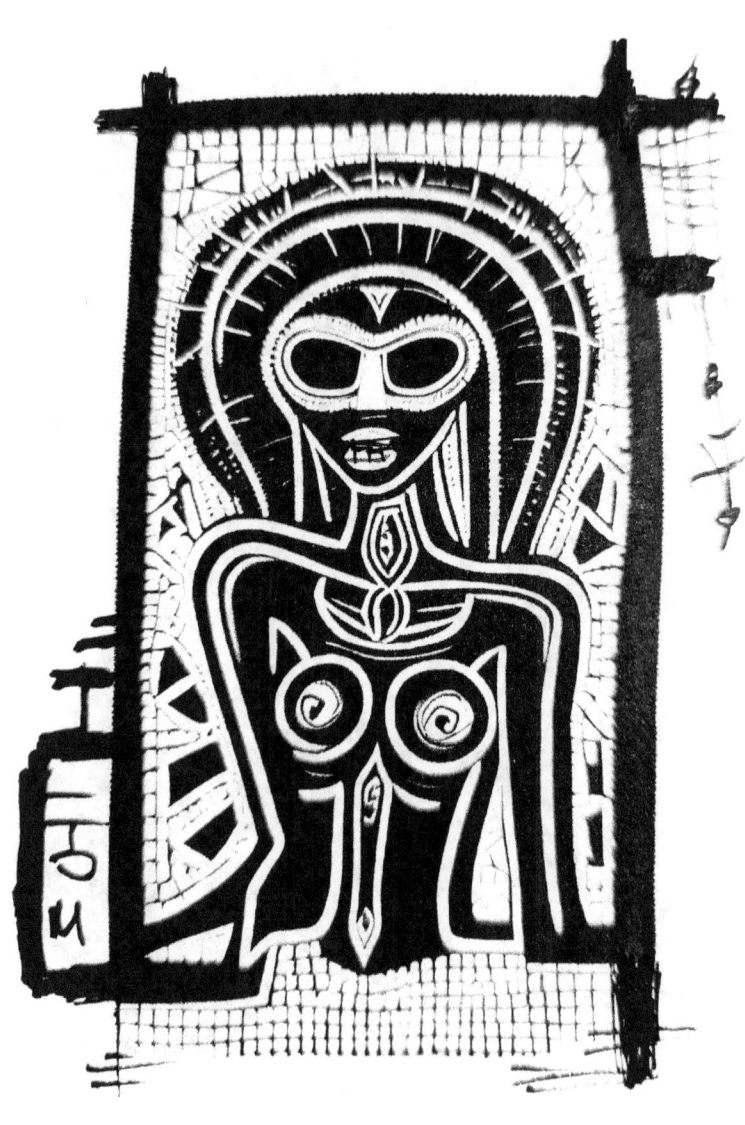

Dreamcatcher. Acrylic Ink Marker on paper. 2024

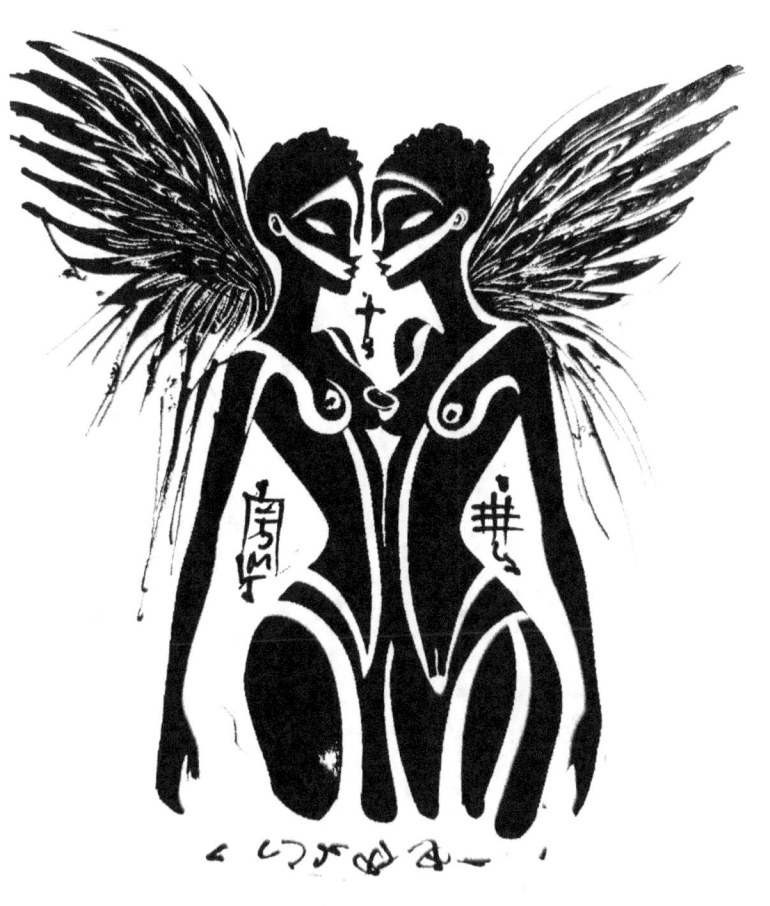

Cherubim. Acrylic Ink Marker on paper. 2024

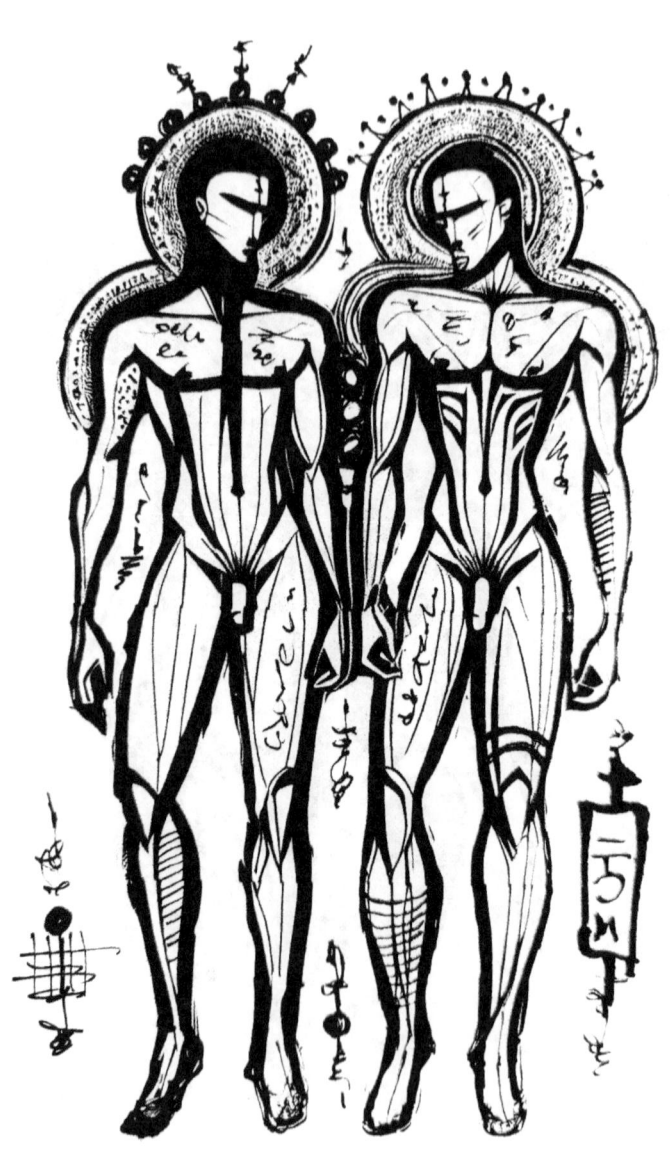

We Two. Acrylic Ink Marker on paper. 2024

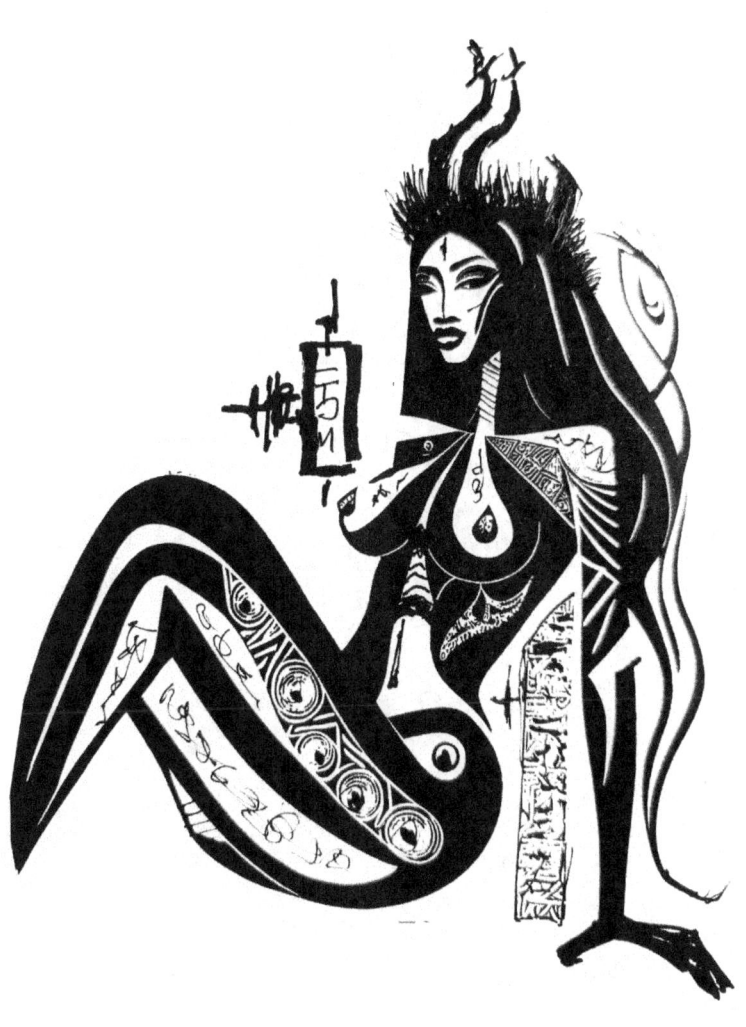

Alisha. Acrylic Ink Marker on paper. 2024

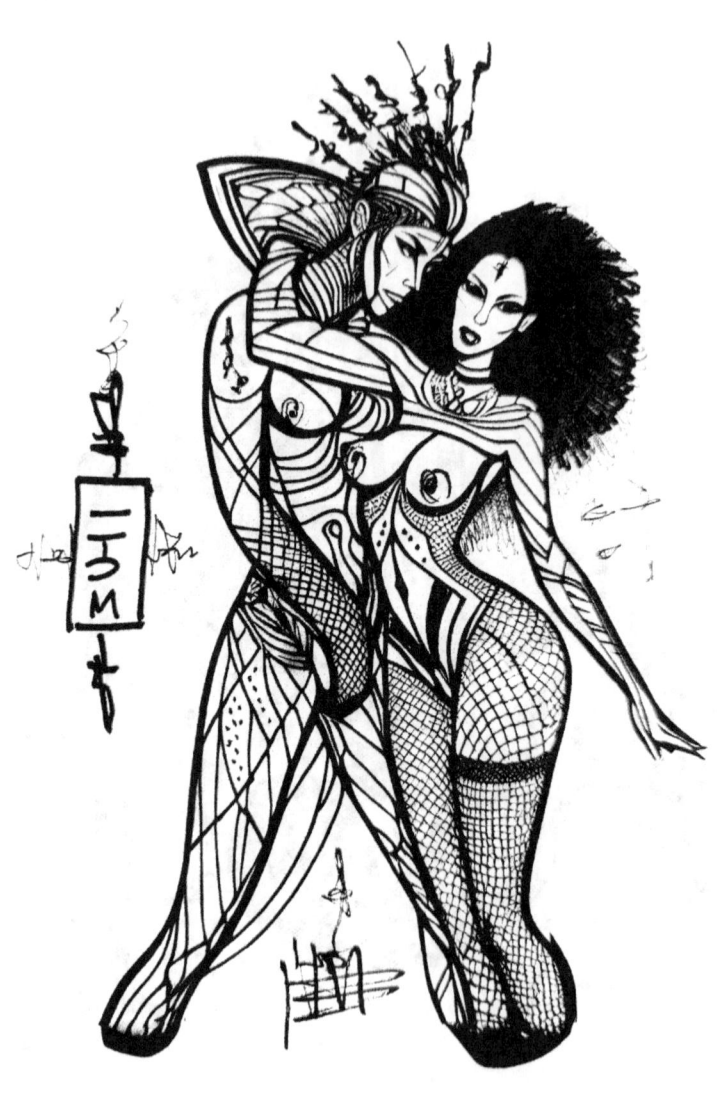

Apollo and Athena. Acrylic Ink Marker on paper. 2024

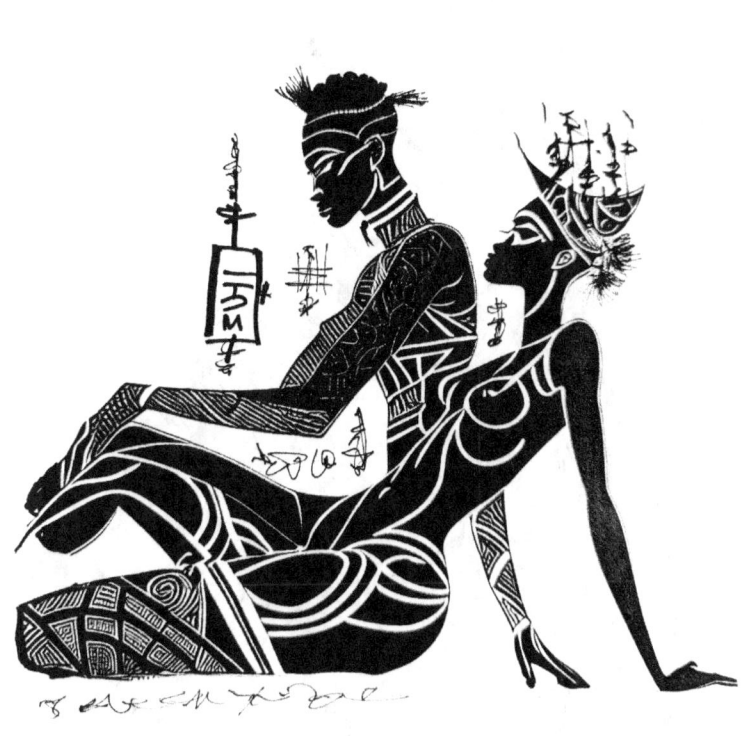

Orishas 3. Acrylic Ink Marker on paper. 2024

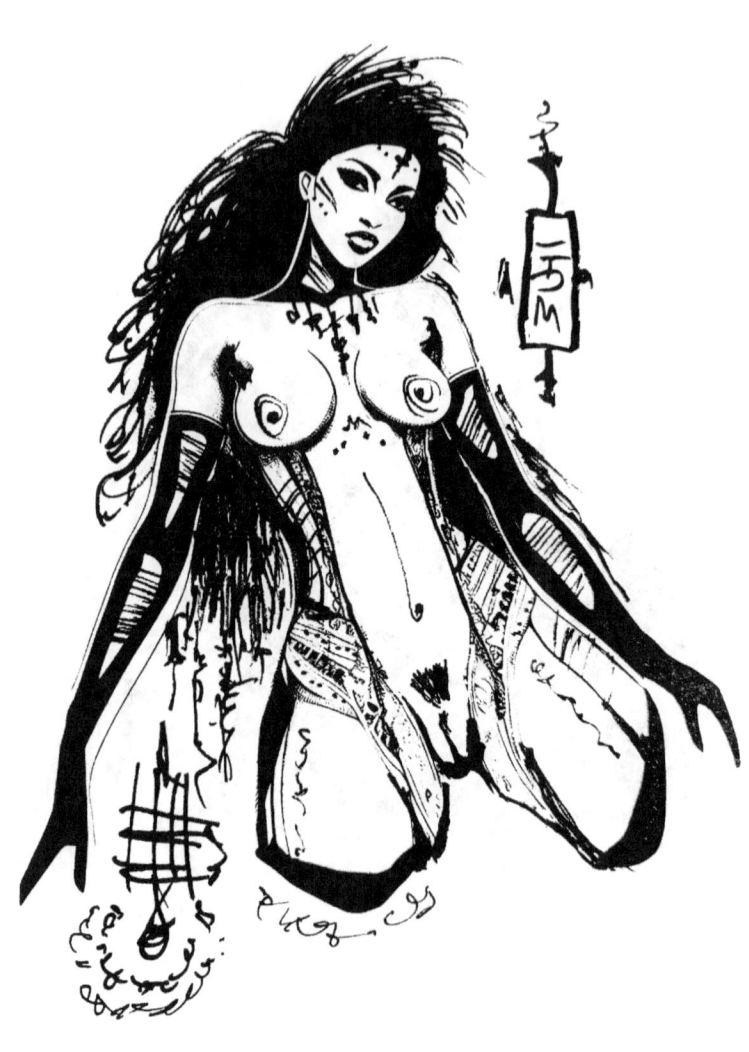

Rose. Acrylic Ink Marker on paper. 2024

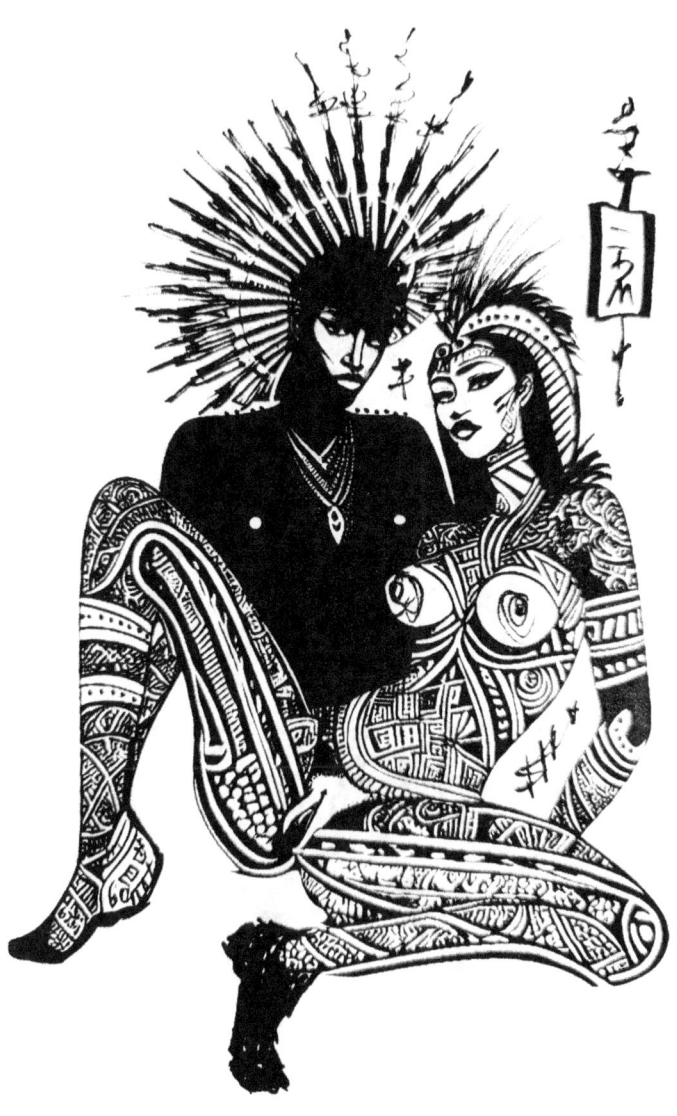

Orishas 5. Acrylic Ink Marker on paper. 2024

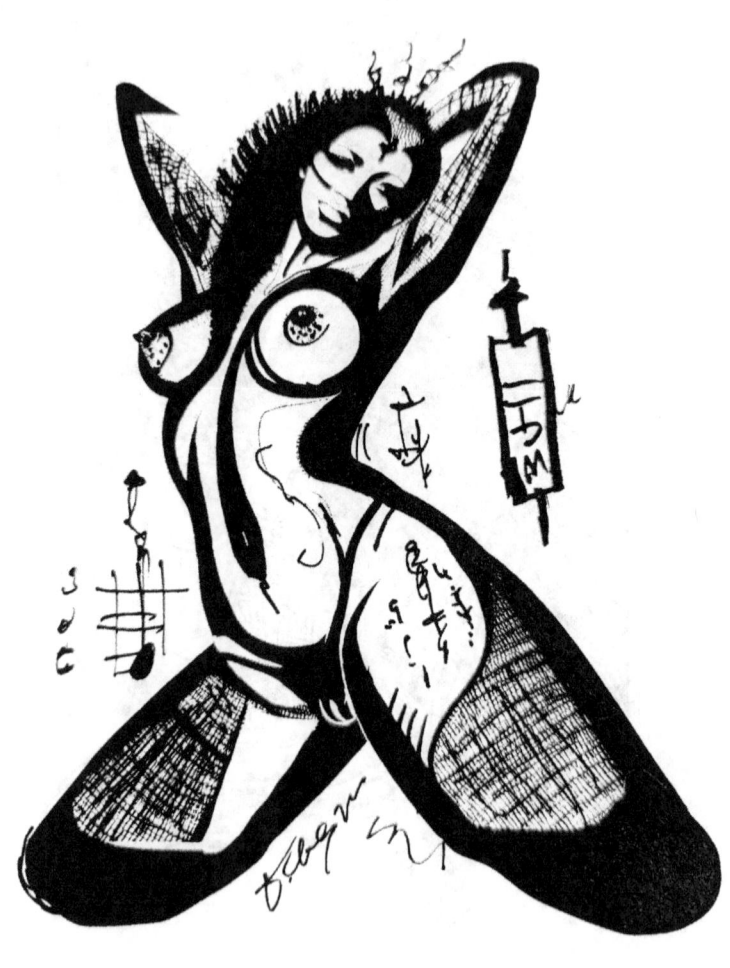

Saturday. Acrylic Ink Marker on paper. 2024

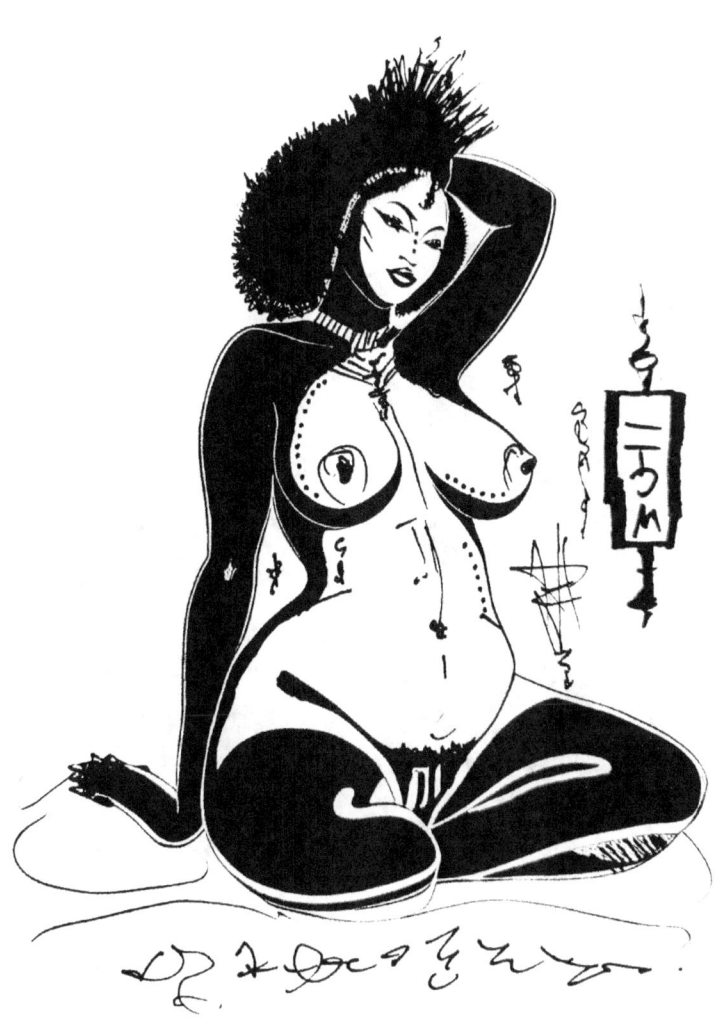

Lust Goddess. Acrylic Ink Marker on paper. 2024

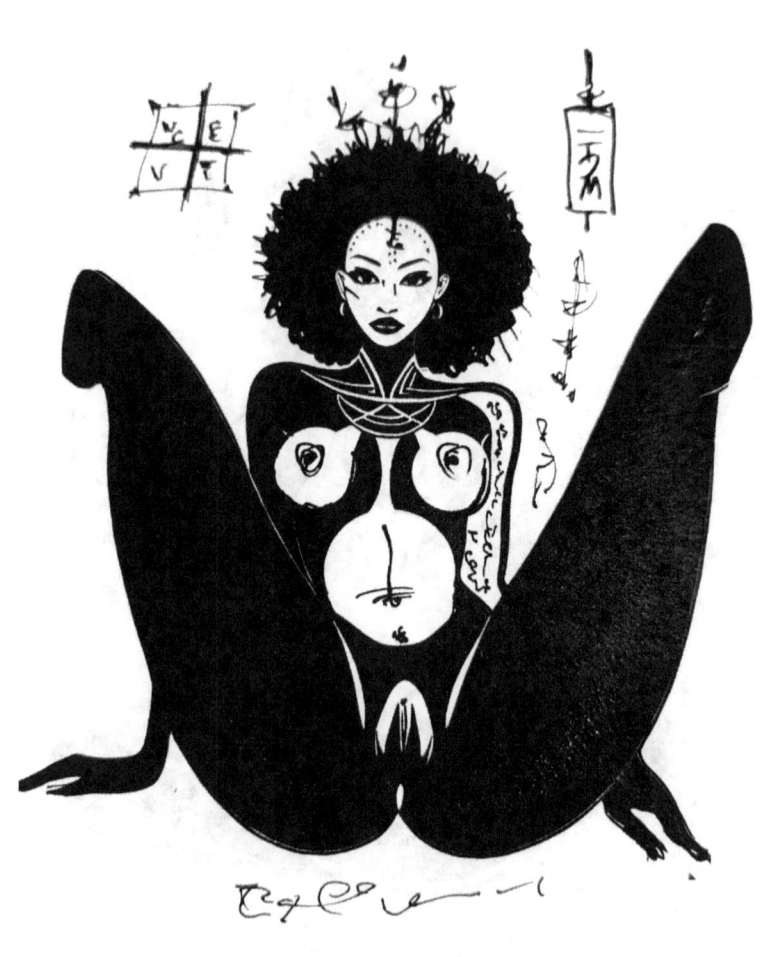

Amandla. Acrylic Ink Marker on paper. 2024

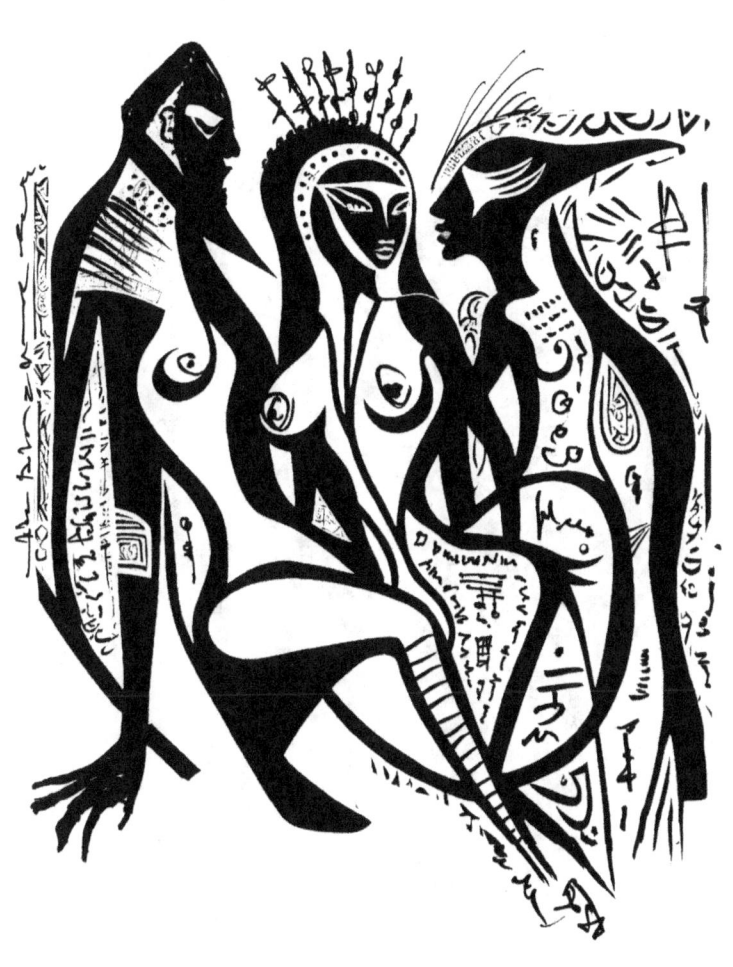

Superheroes. Acrylic Ink Marker on paper. 2024

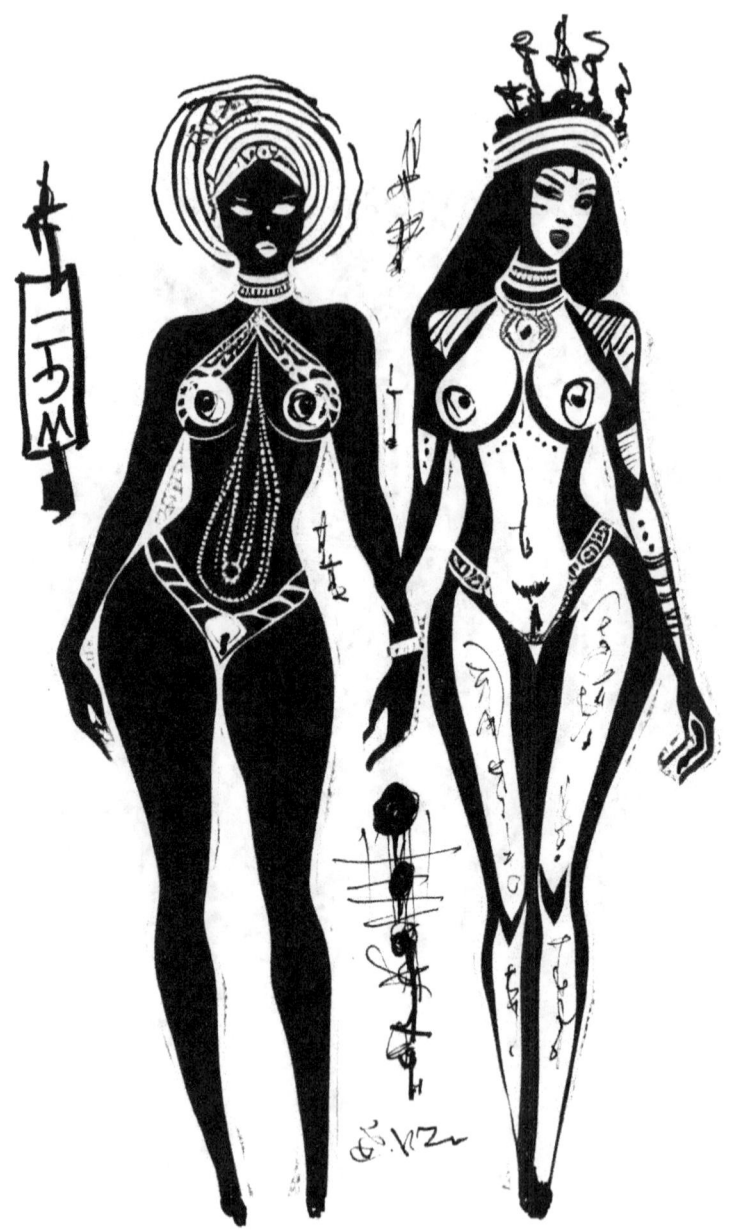

Found. Acrylic Ink Marker on paper. 2024

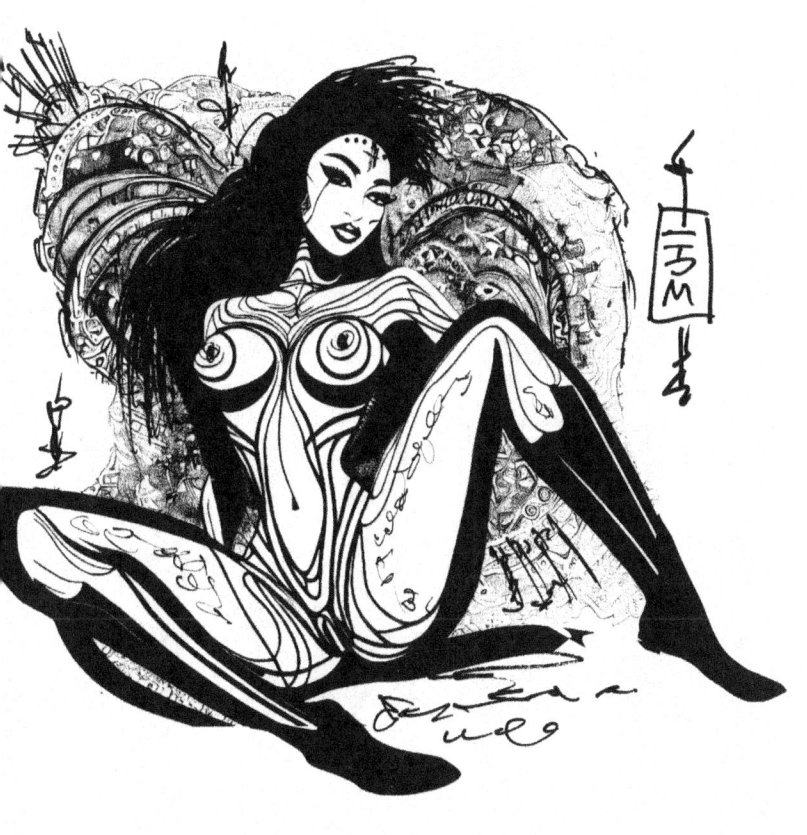

The Portal. Acrylic Ink Marker on paper. 2024

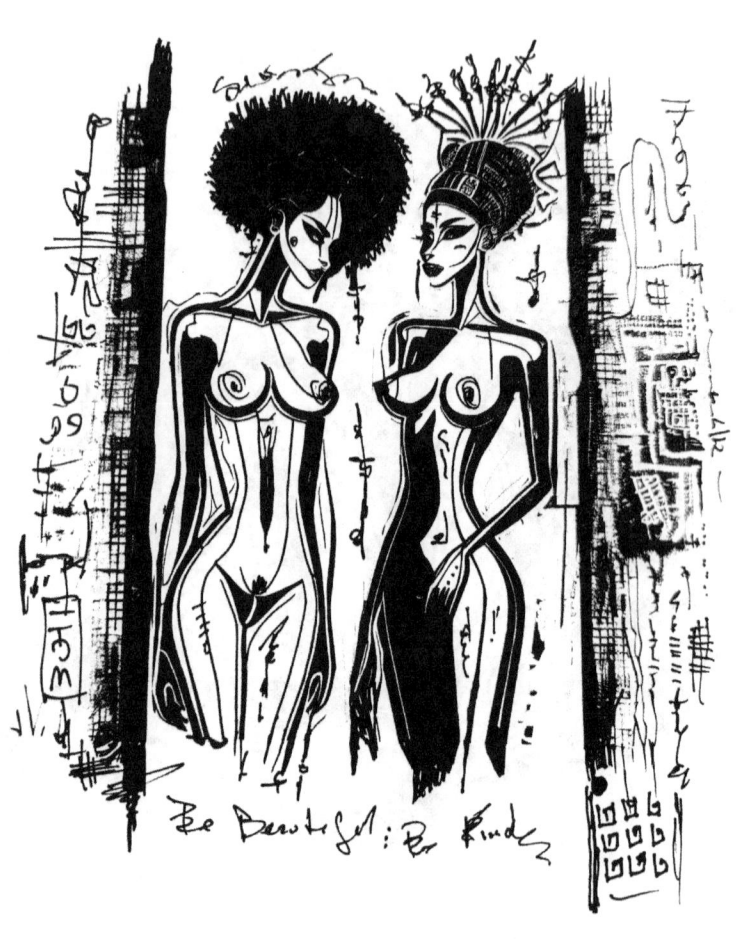

Beautiful Kind. Acrylic Ink Marker on paper. 2024

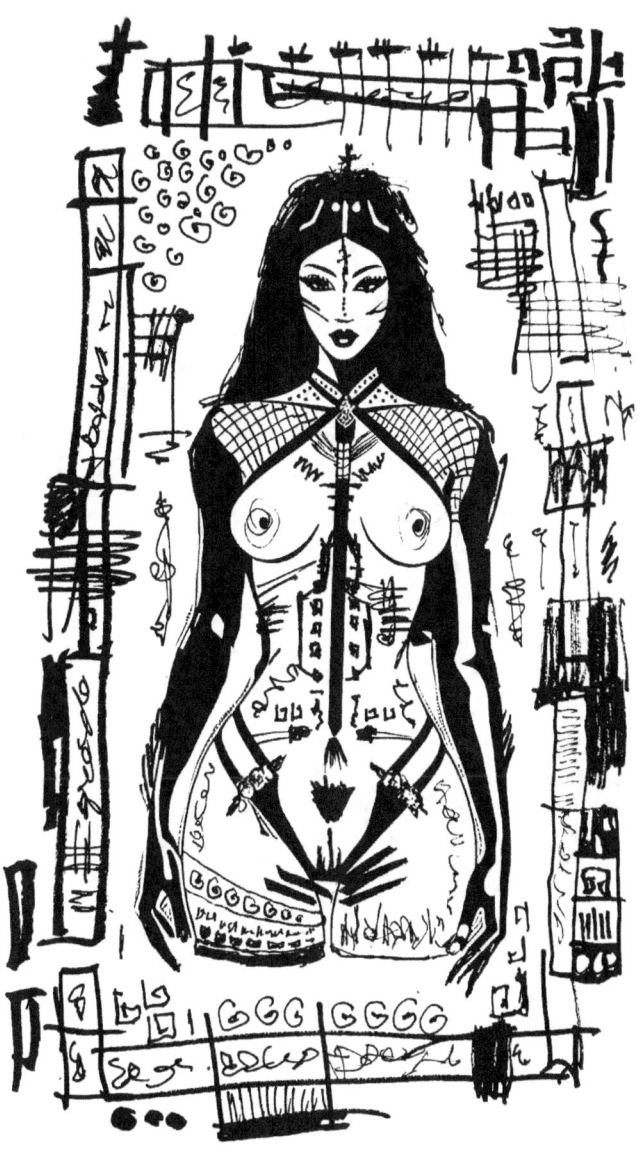

The Mirror. Acrylic Ink Marker on paper. 2024

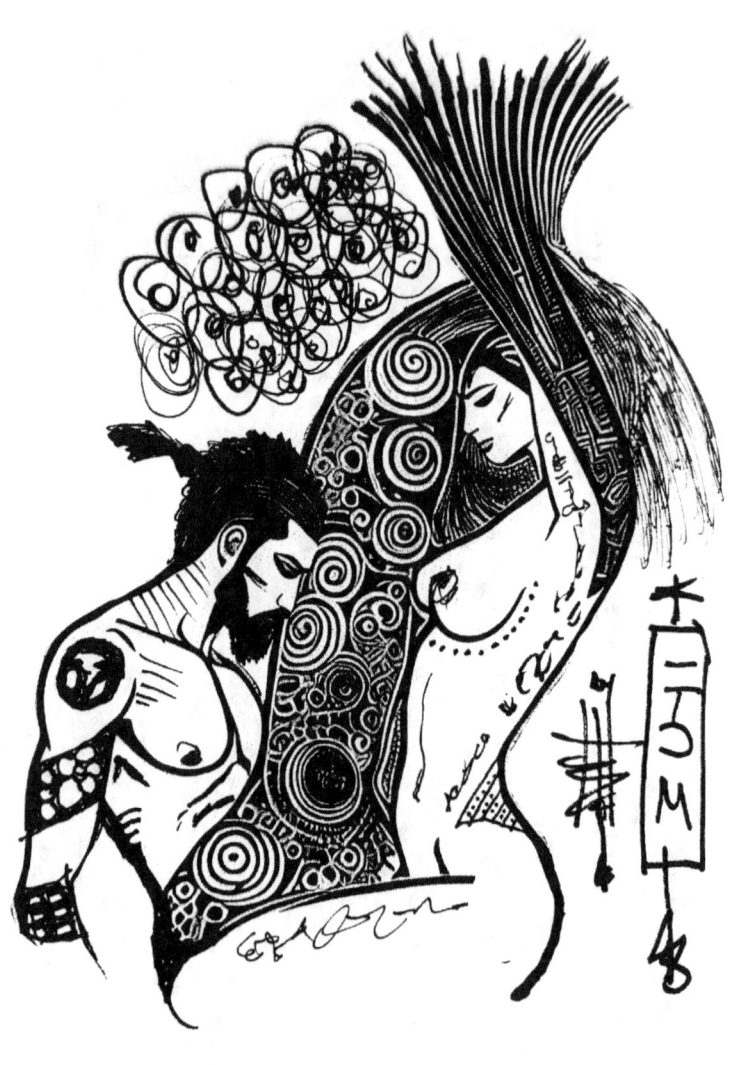

The Sash. Acrylic Ink Marker on paper. 2024

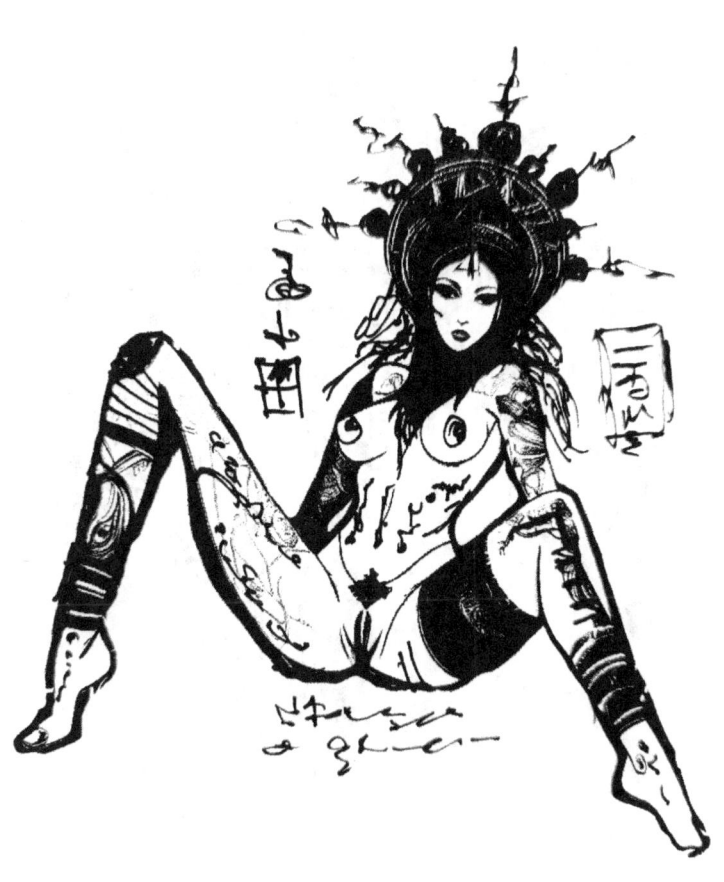

Cree. Acrylic Ink Marker on paper. 2024

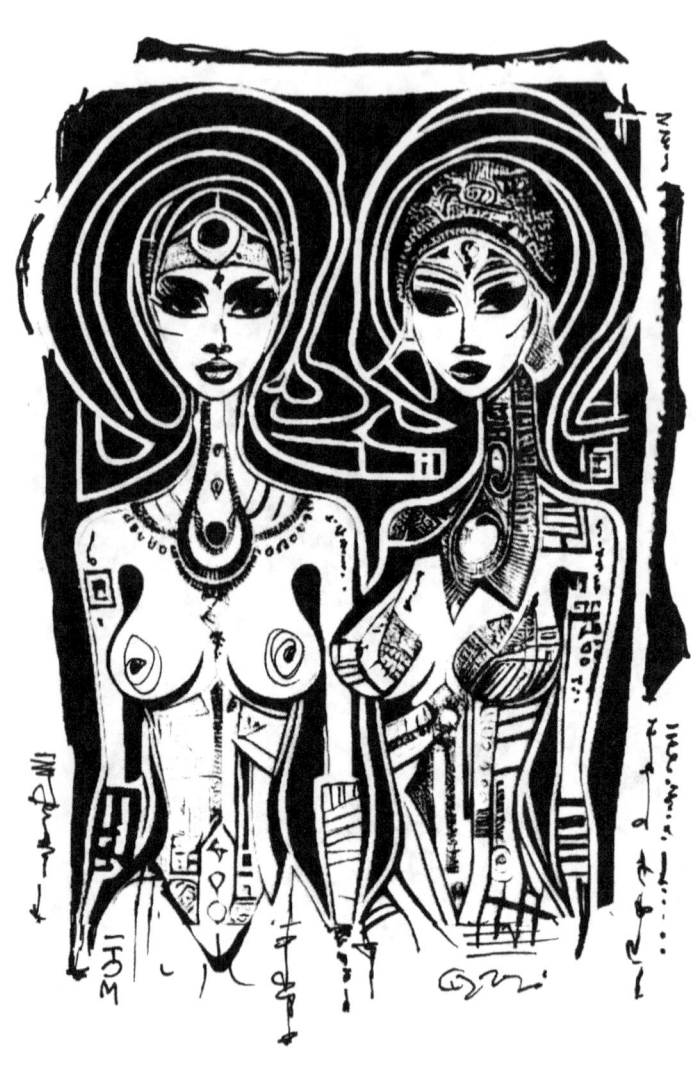

Visitors Acrylic Ink Marker on paper. 2024

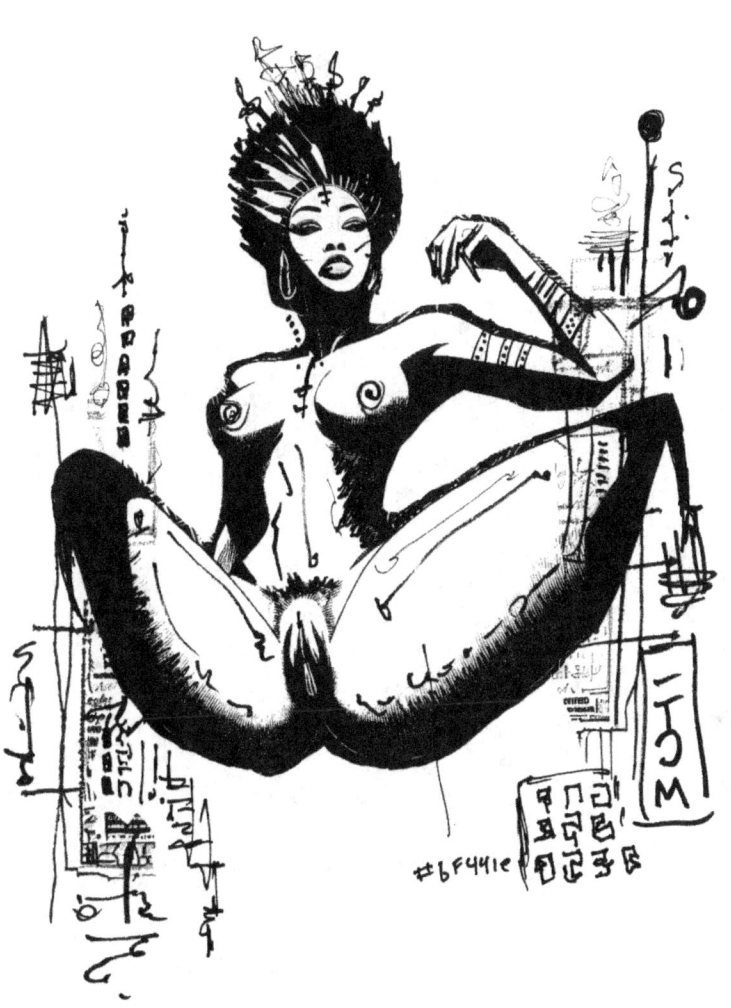

Quantum. Acrylic Ink Marker on paper. 2024

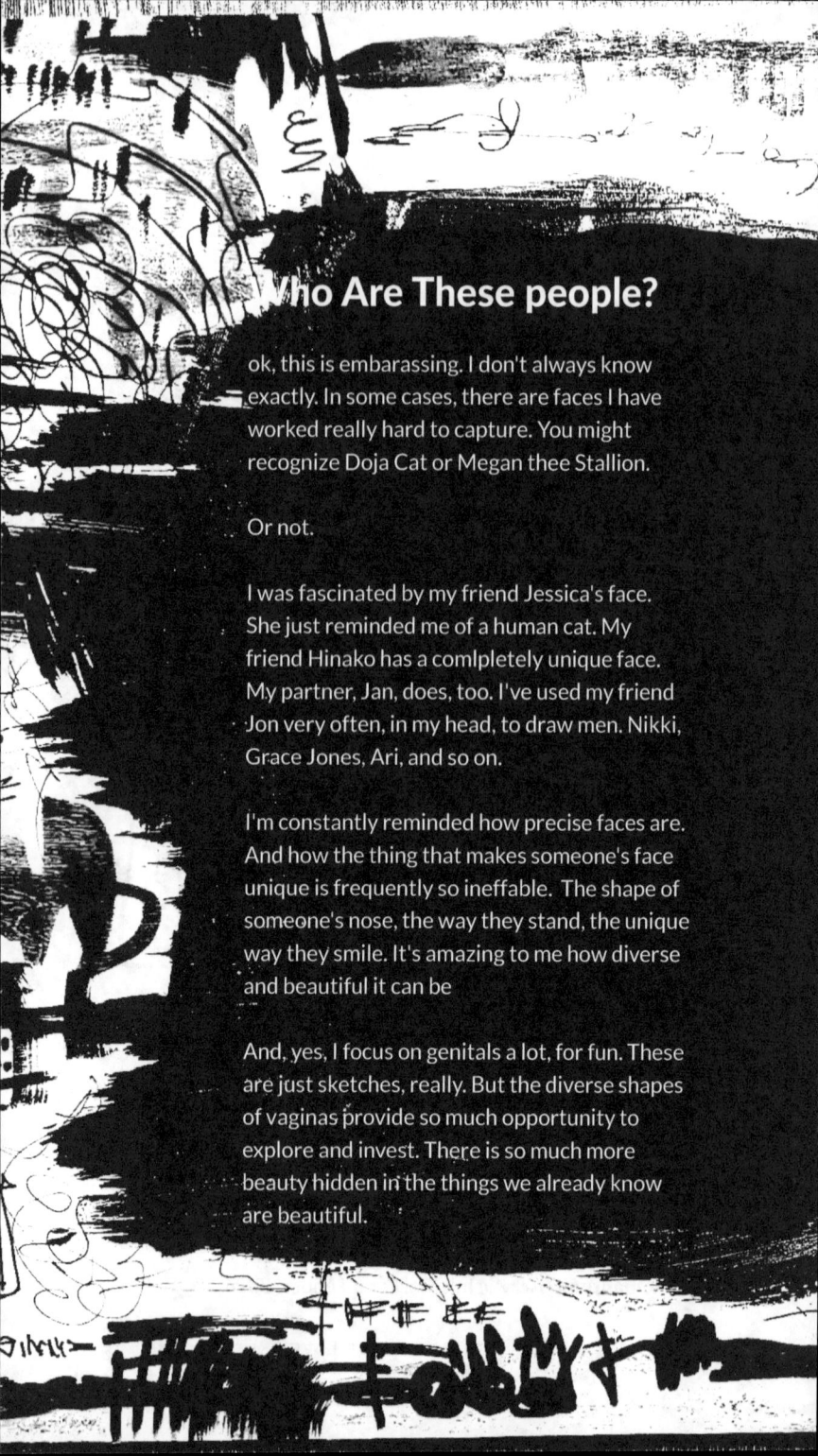

Who Are These people?

ok, this is embarassing. I don't always know exactly. In some cases, there are faces I have worked really hard to capture. You might recognize Doja Cat or Megan thee Stallion.

Or not.

I was fascinated by my friend Jessica's face. She just reminded me of a human cat. My friend Hinako has a comlpletely unique face. My partner, Jan, does, too. I've used my friend Jon very often, in my head, to draw men. Nikki, Grace Jones, Ari, and so on.

I'm constantly reminded how precise faces are. And how the thing that makes someone's face unique is frequently so ineffable. The shape of someone's nose, the way they stand, the unique way they smile. It's amazing to me how diverse and beautiful it can be

And, yes, I focus on genitals a lot, for fun. These are just sketches, really. But the diverse shapes of vaginas provide so much opportunity to explore and invest. There is so much more beauty hidden in the things we already know are beautiful.

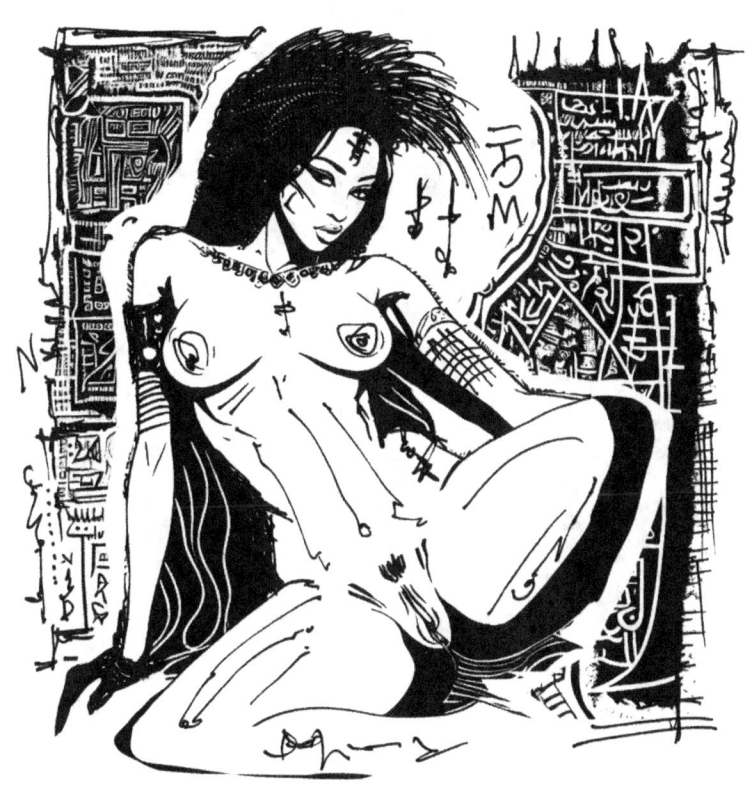

Cognac Queen. Acrylic Ink Marker on paper. 2024

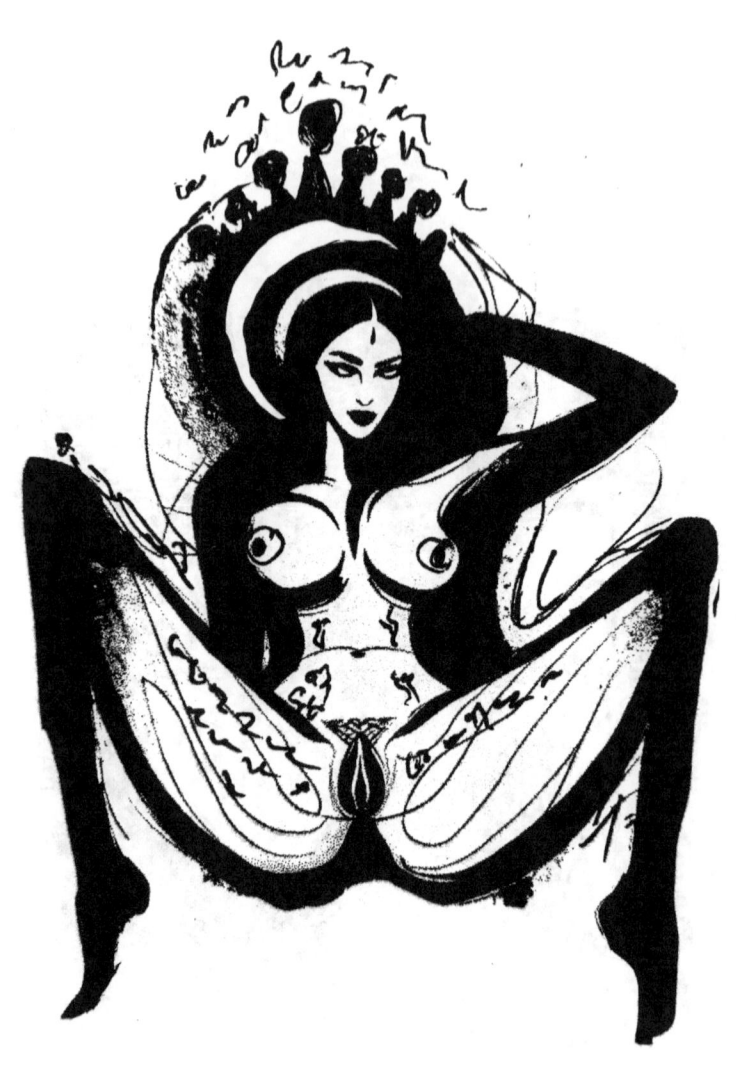

Super. Acrylic Ink Marker on paper. 2024

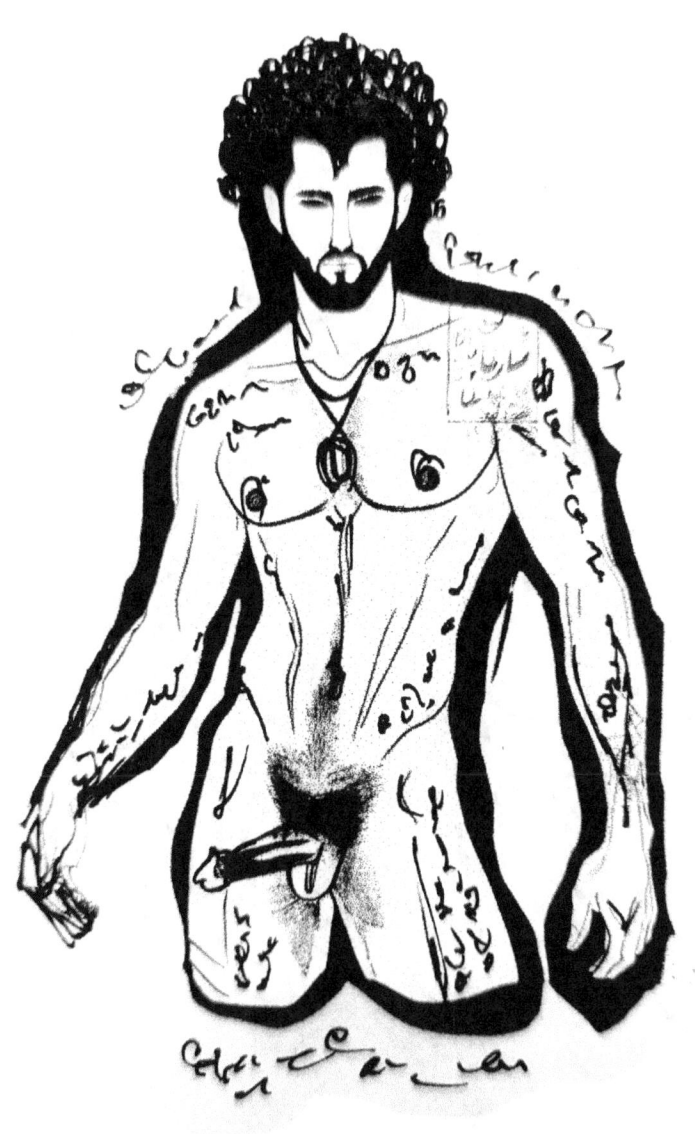

Helado. Acrylic Ink Marker on paper. 2024

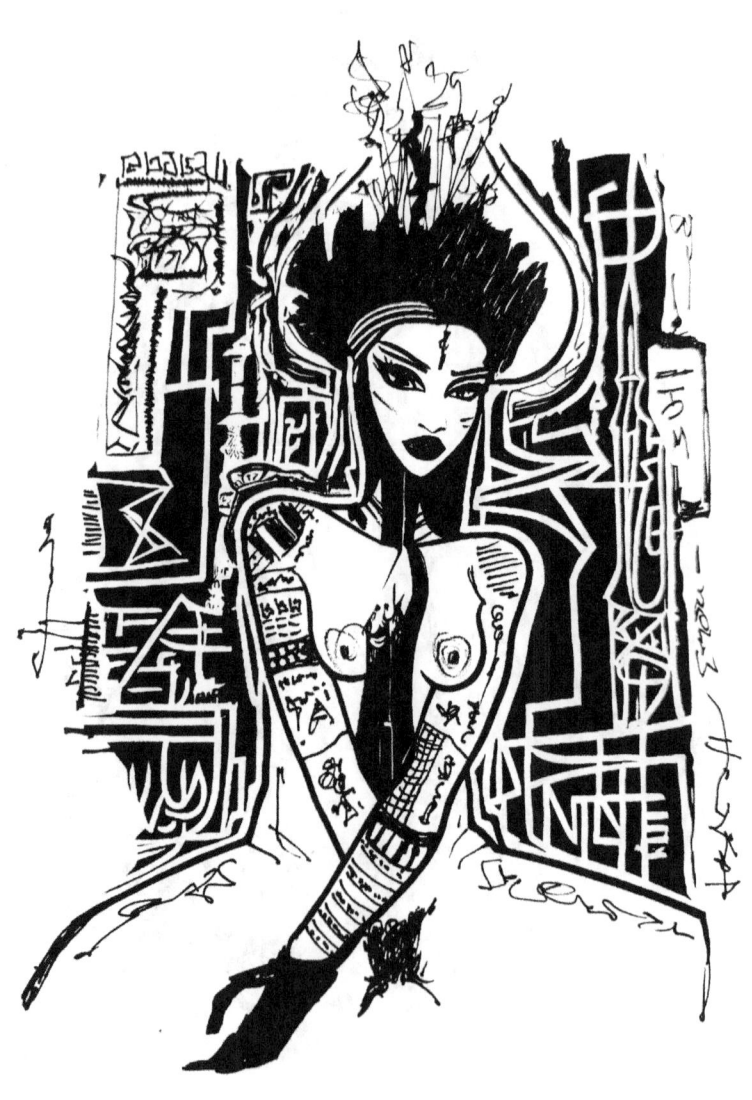

Precious. Acrylic Ink Marker on paper. 2024

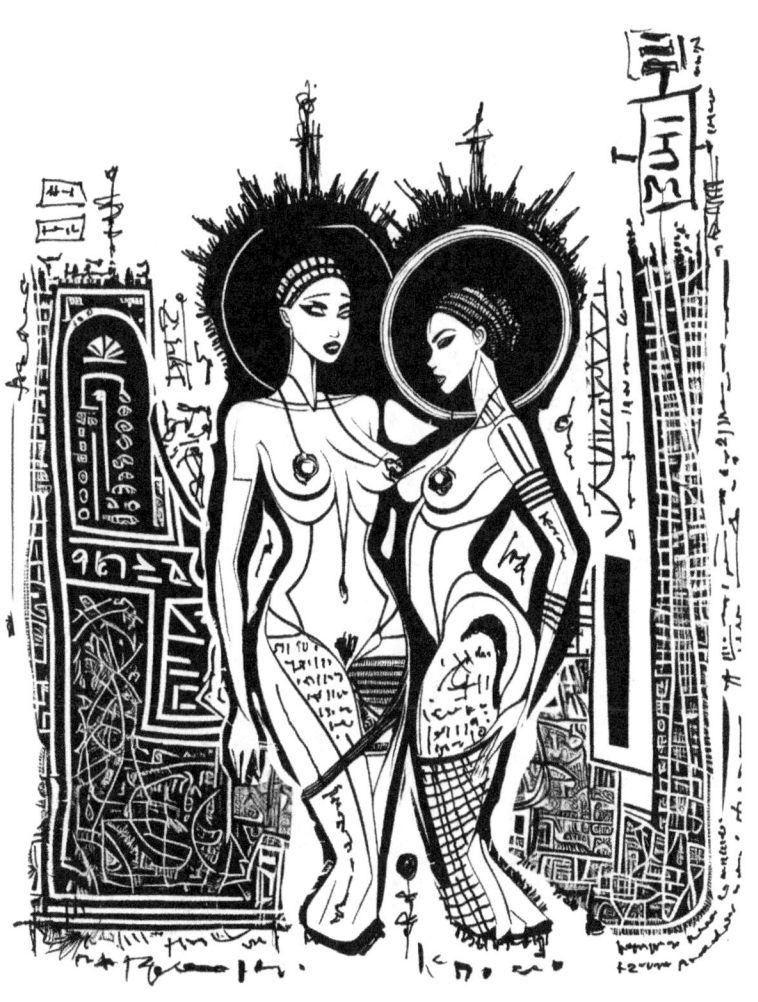

City Girls. Acrylic Ink Marker on paper. 2024

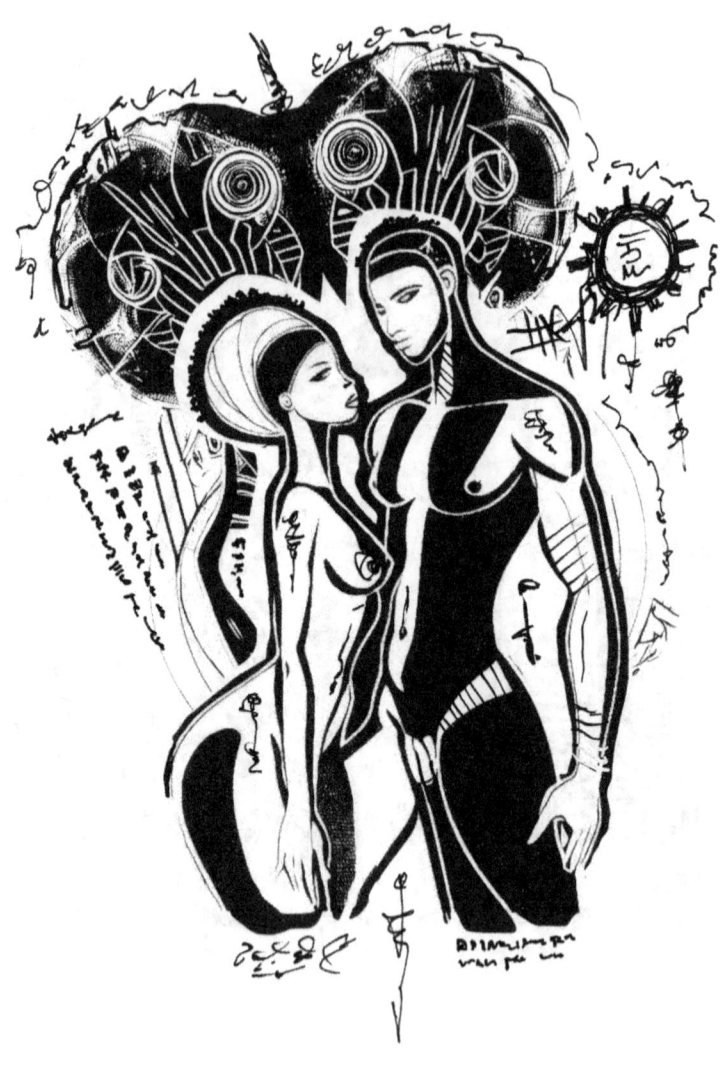

Planetary. Acrylic Ink Marker on paper. 2024

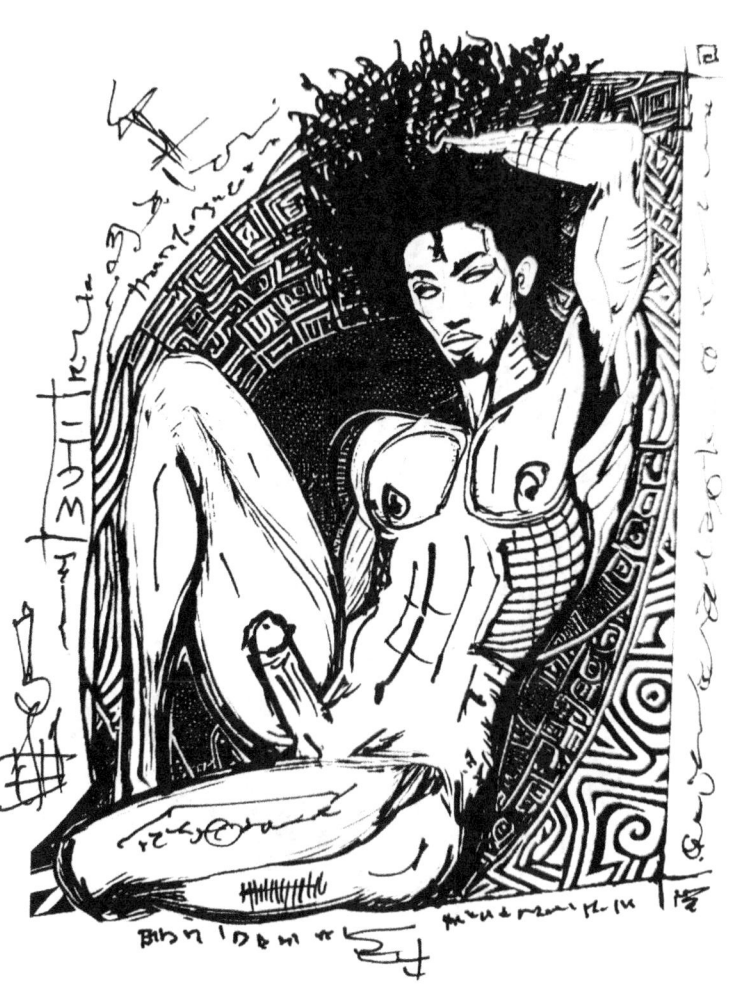

Eli. Acrylic Ink Marker on paper. 2024

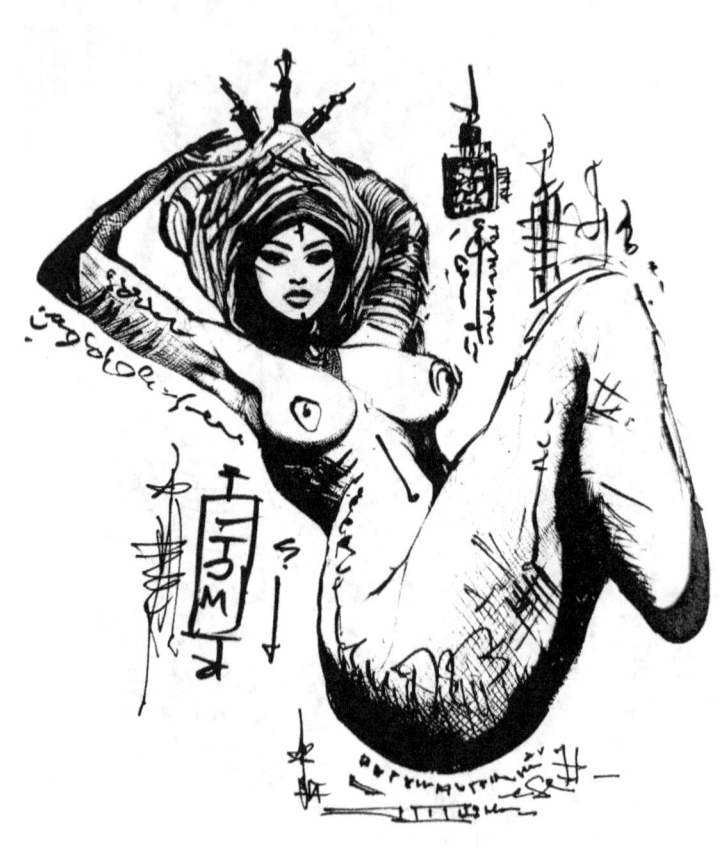

Shay. Acrylic Ink Marker on paper. 2024

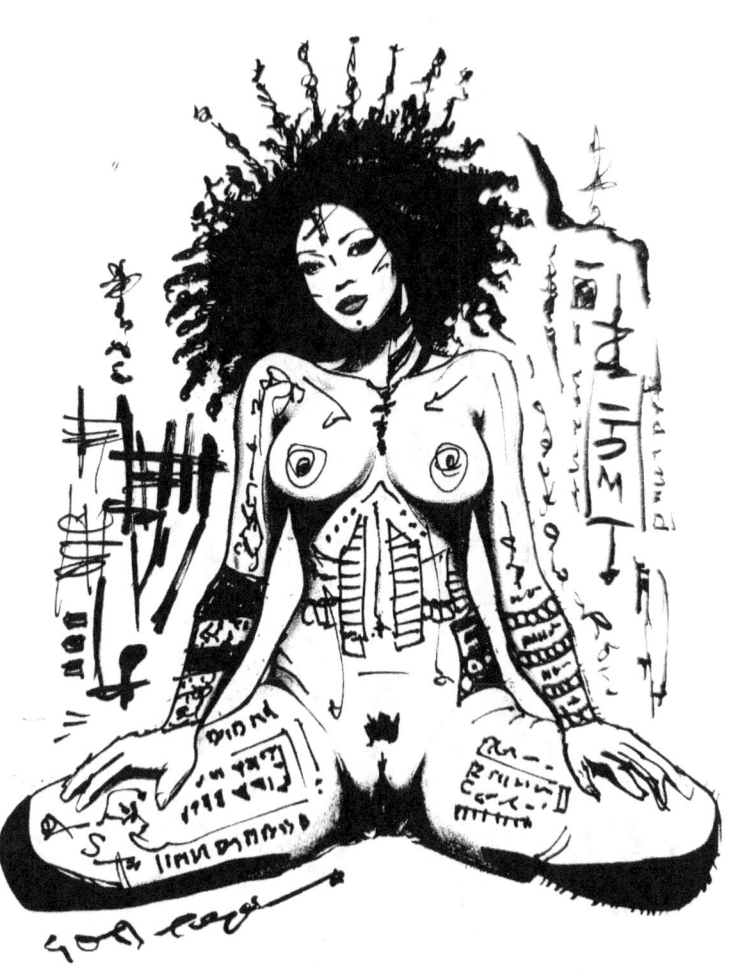

Diana. Acrylic Ink Marker on paper. 2024

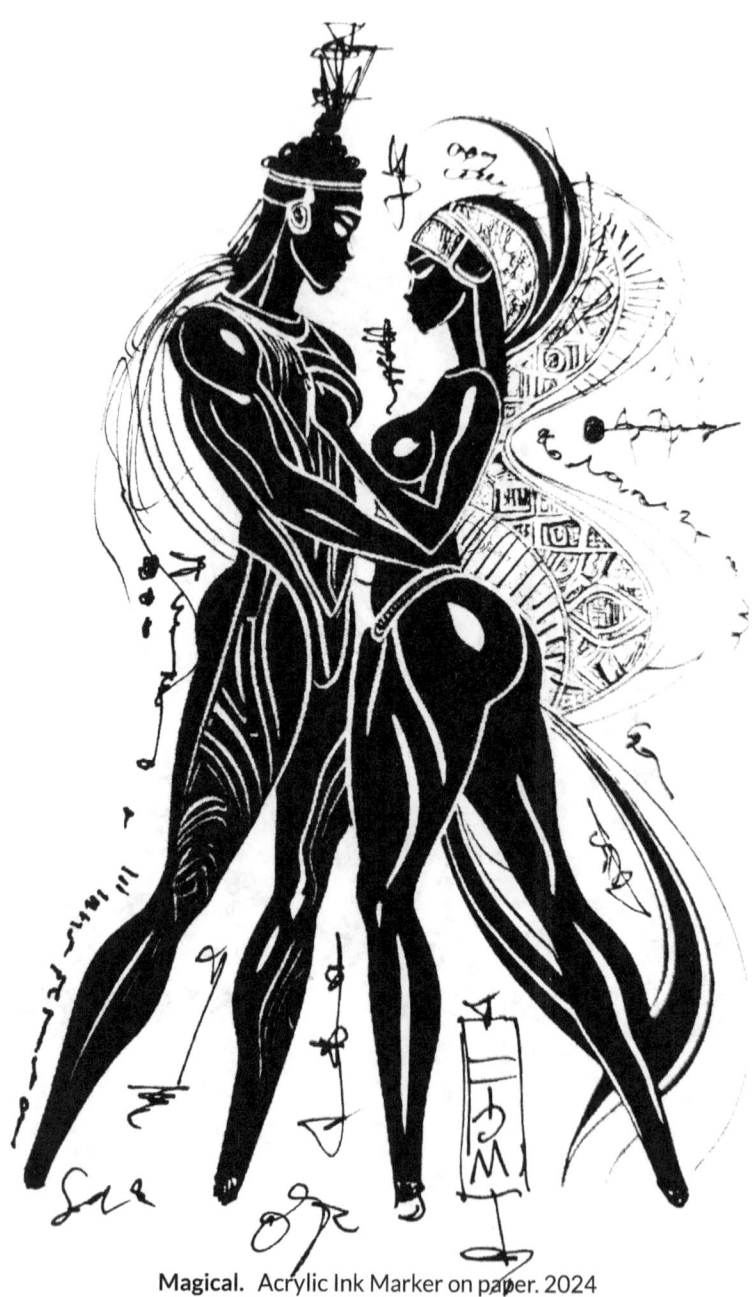

Magical. Acrylic Ink Marker on paper. 2024

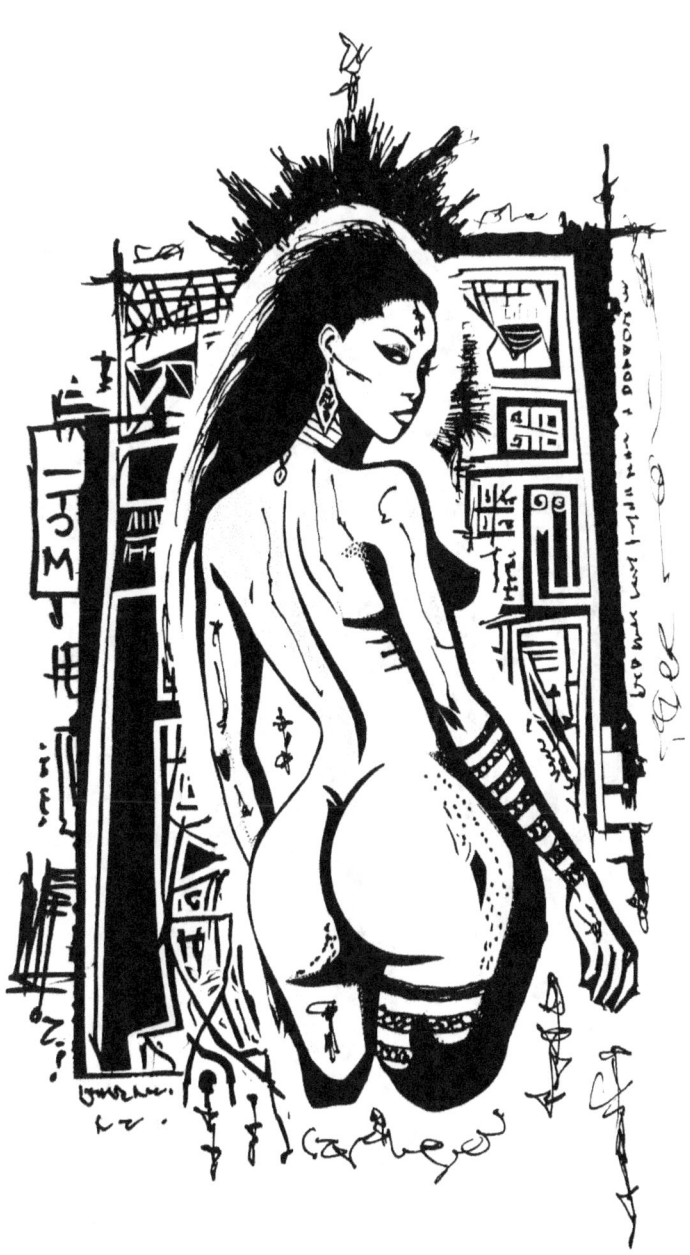

From the Closet. Acrylic Ink Marker on paper. 2024

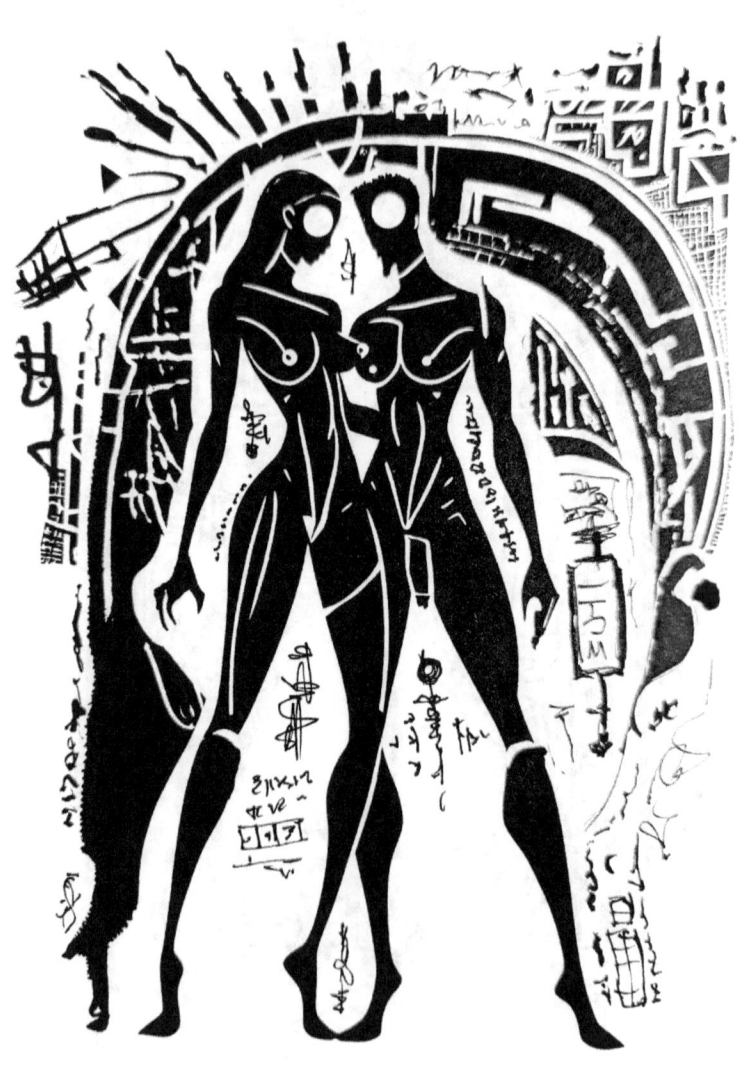

Eyes of the City. Acrylic Ink Marker on paper. 2024

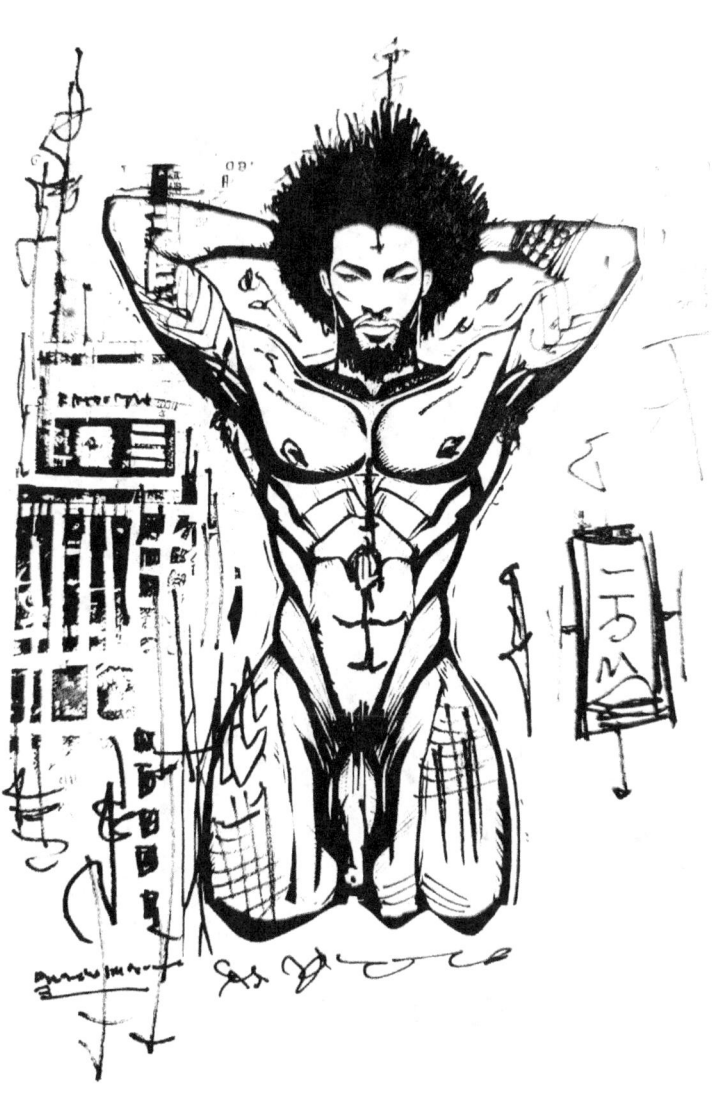

At the Gym. Acrylic Ink Marker on paper. 2024

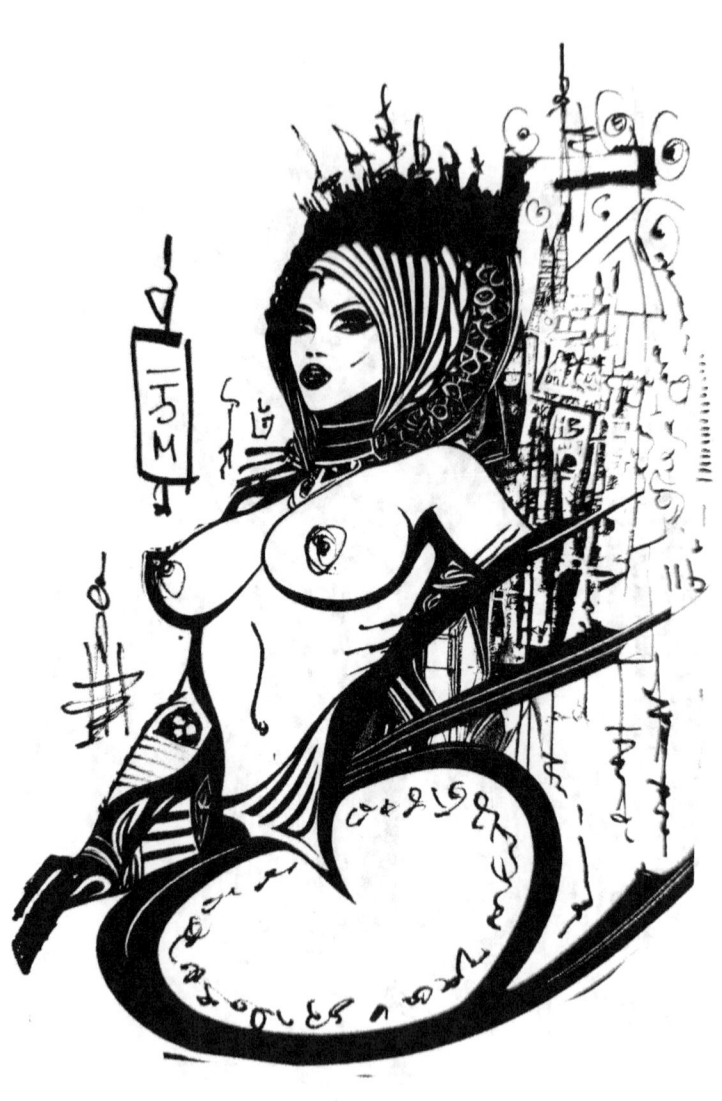

Cosmopolitan. Acrylic Ink Marker on paper. 2024

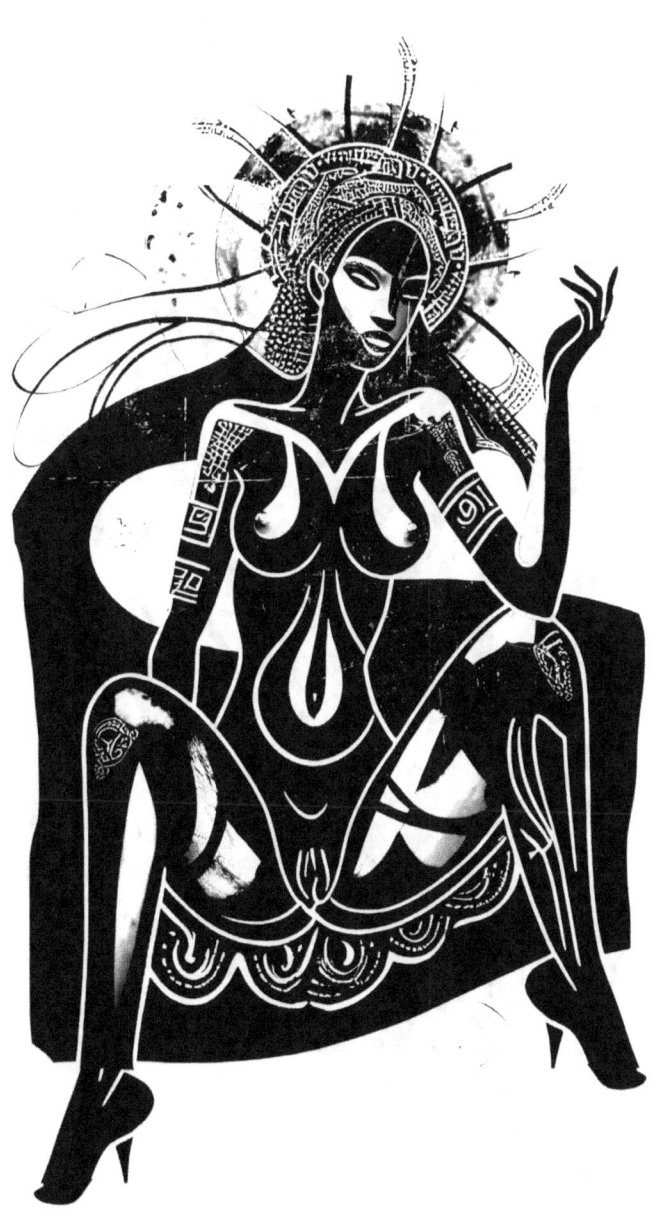

Fearless. Acrylic Ink Marker on paper. 2021

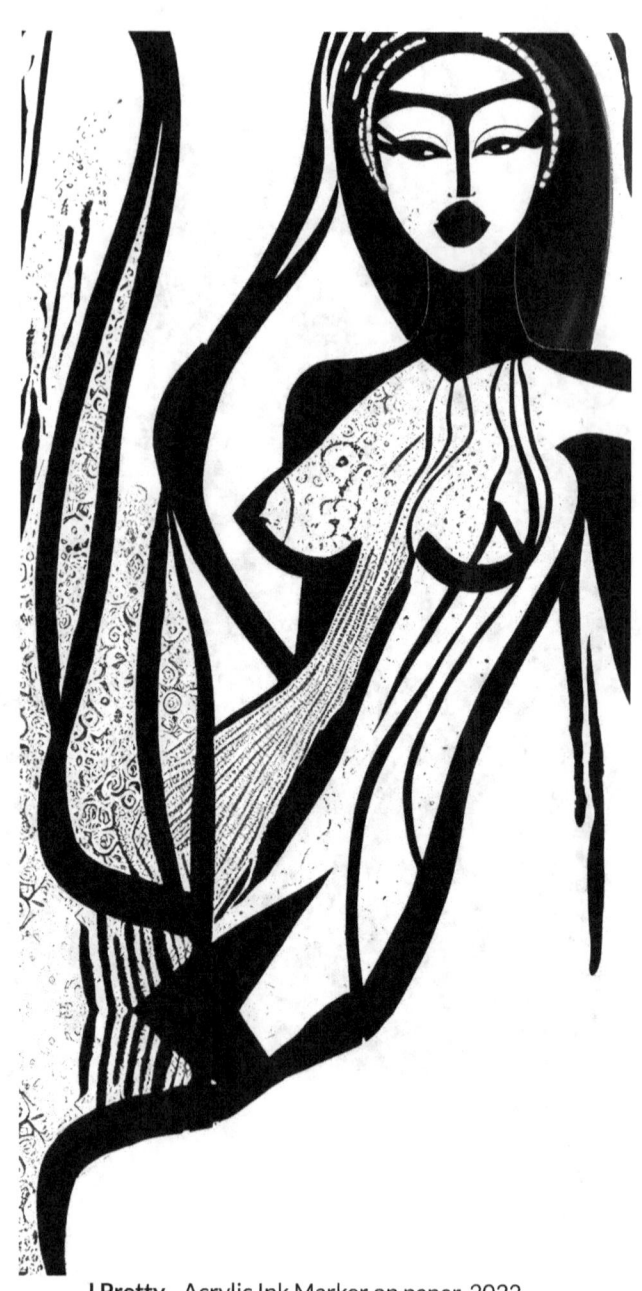

I Pretty. Acrylic Ink Marker on paper. 2022

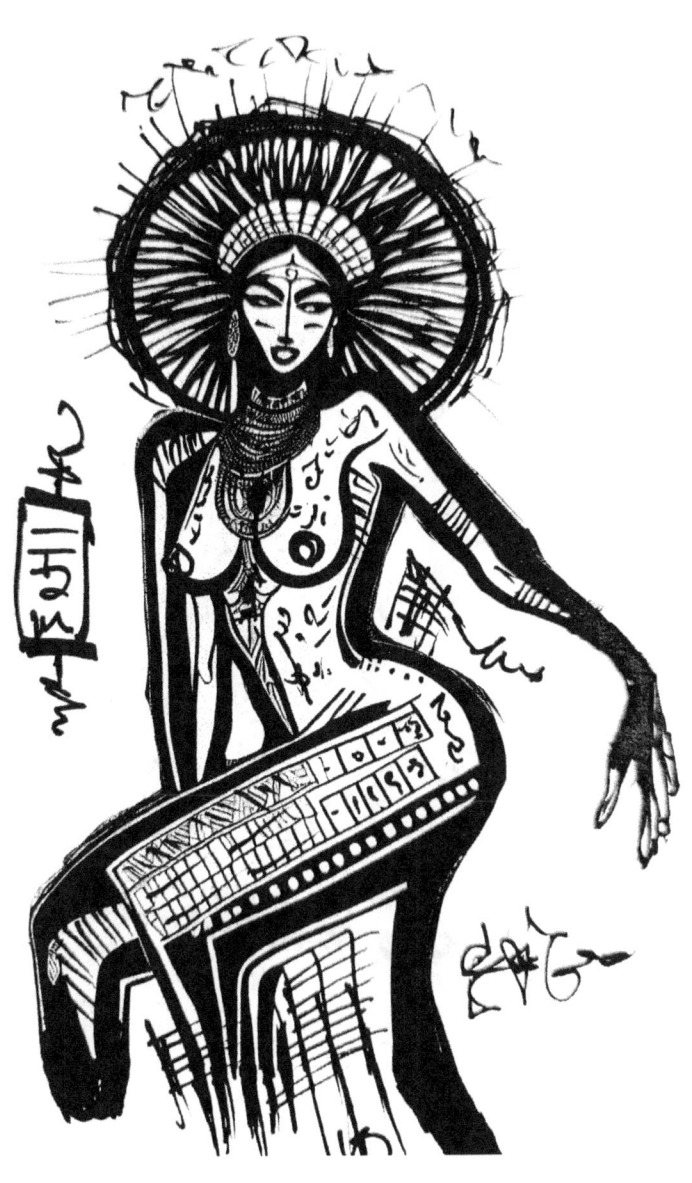

Sun Dance. Acrylic Ink Marker on paper. 2023

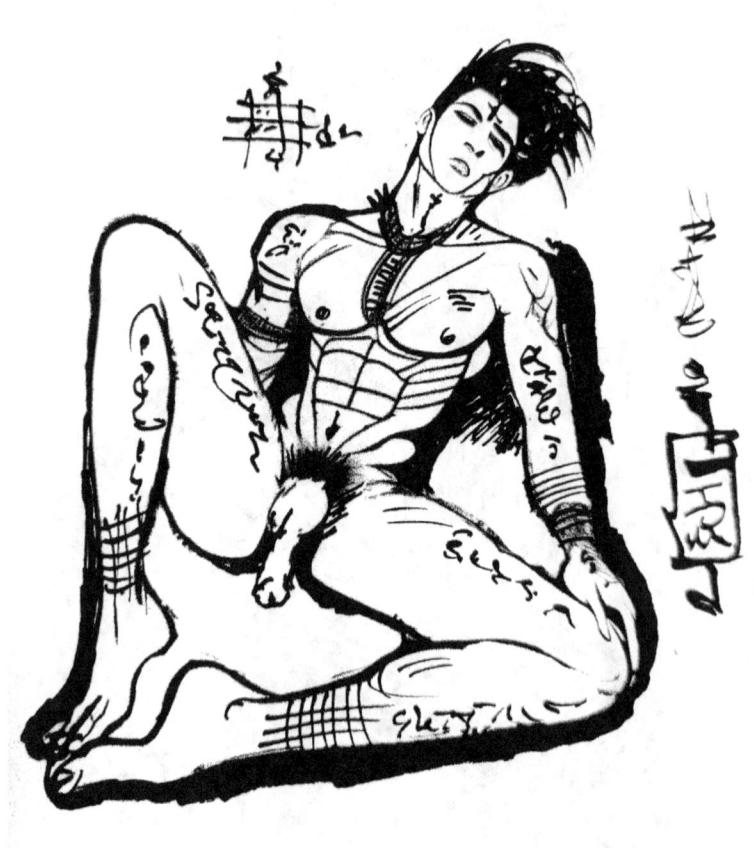

Arise. Acrylic Ink Marker on paper. 2024

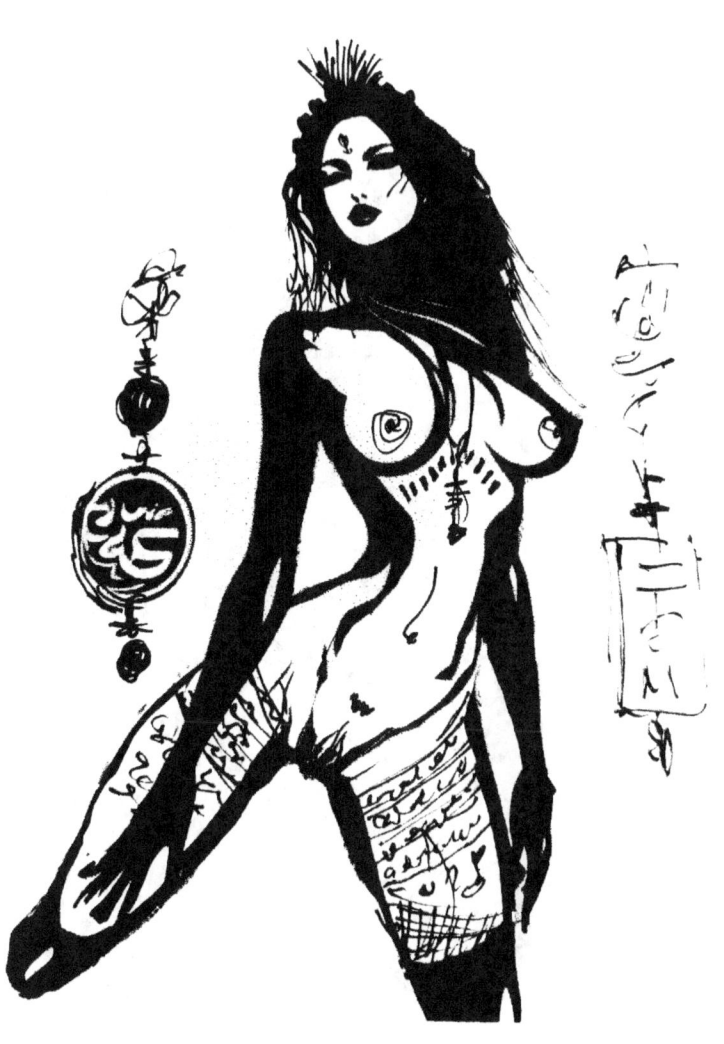

Carly. Acrylic Ink Marker on paper. 2022

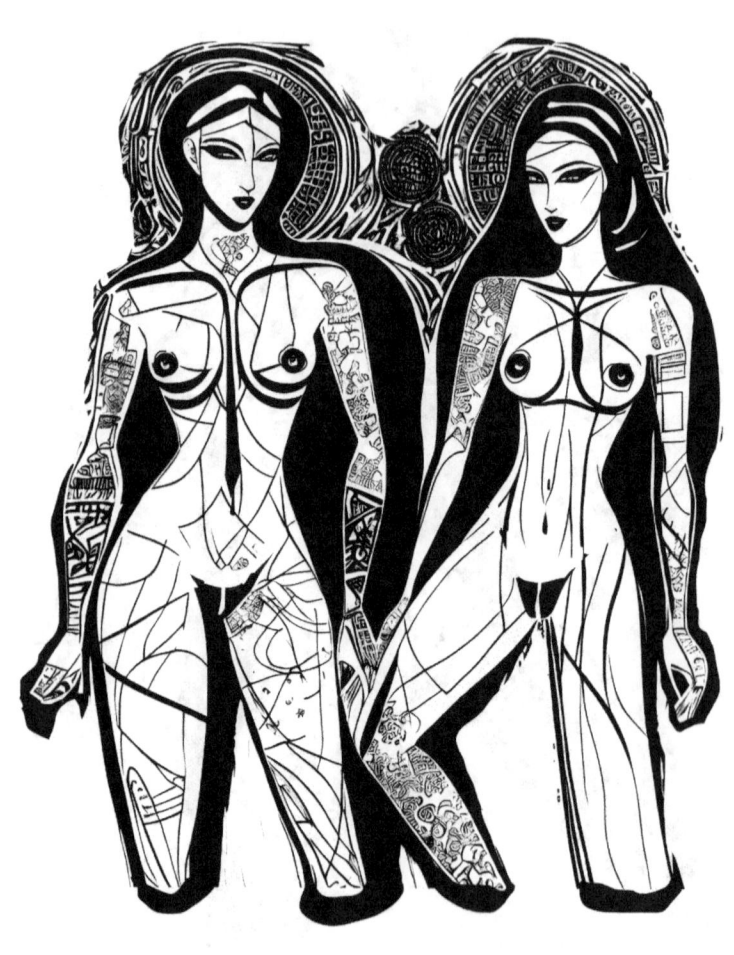

The Yarn Sisters. Acrylic Ink Marker on paper. 2022

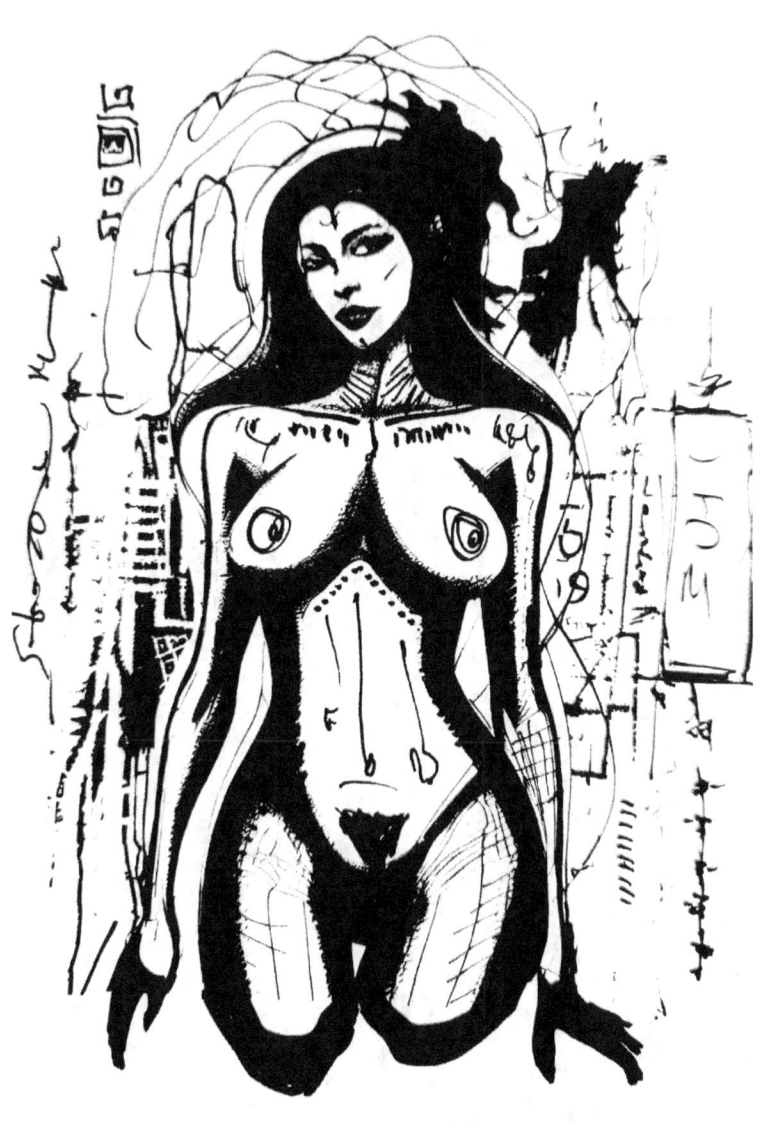

Hannah. Acrylic Ink Marker on paper. 2024

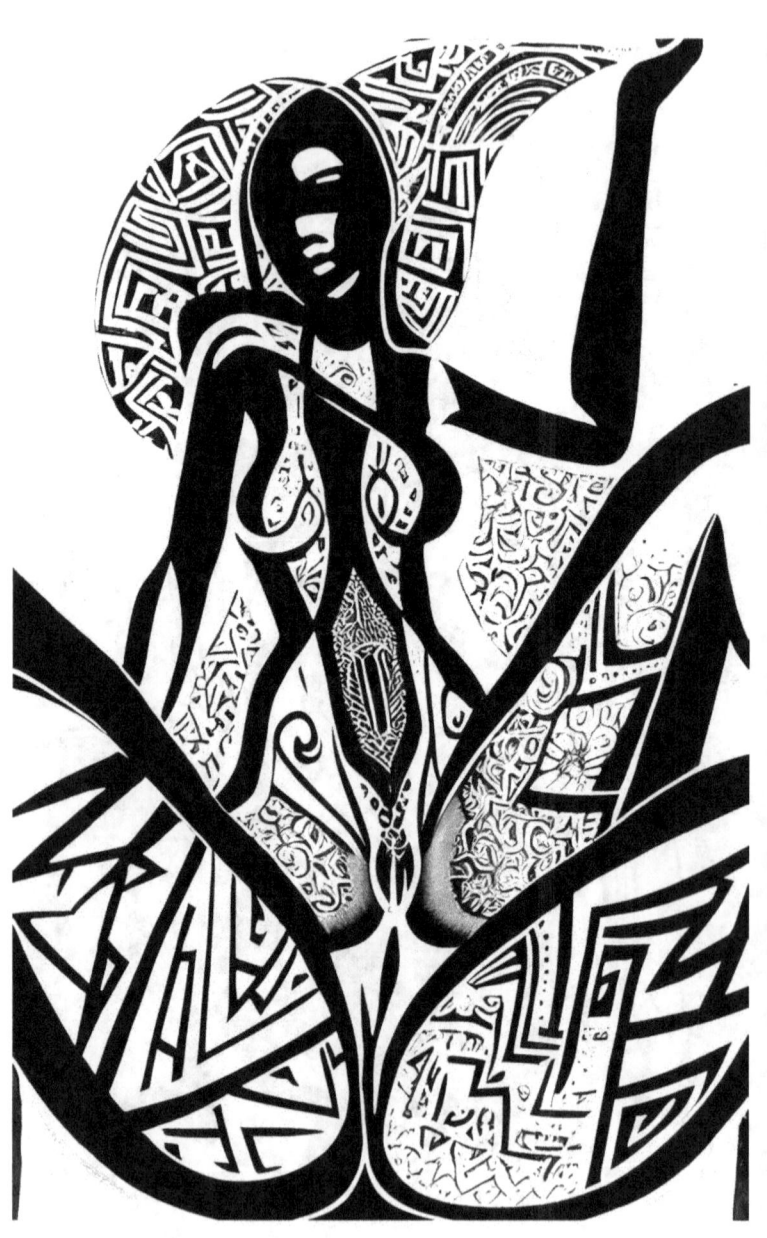

Unify. Acrylic Ink Marker on paper. 2021

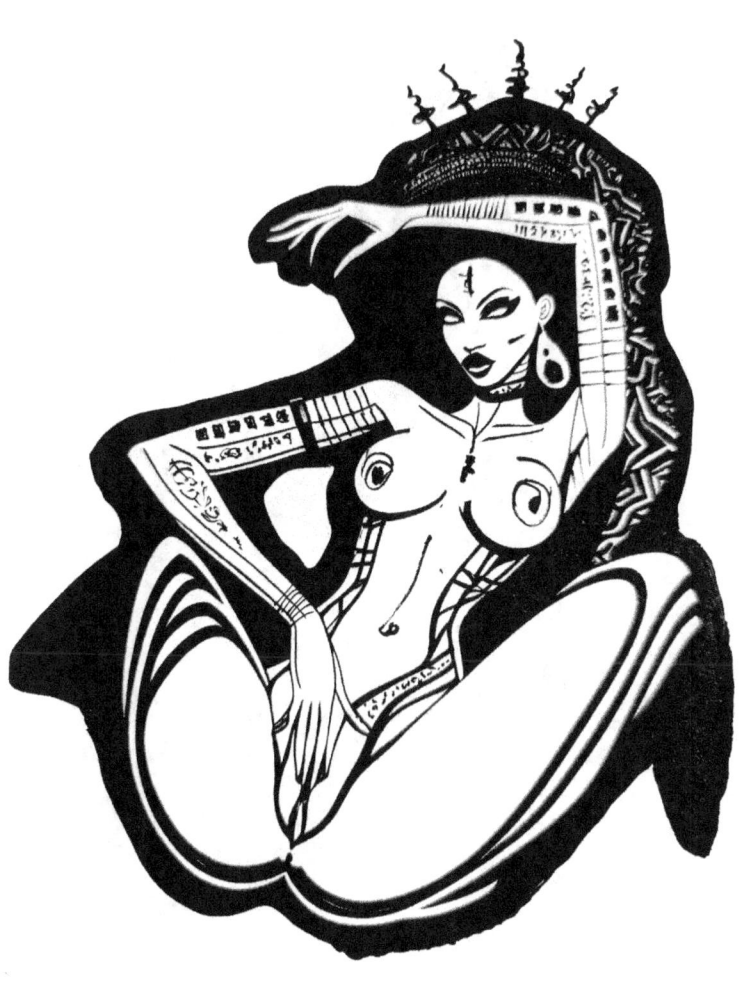

Janelle. Acrylic Ink Marker on paper. 2024

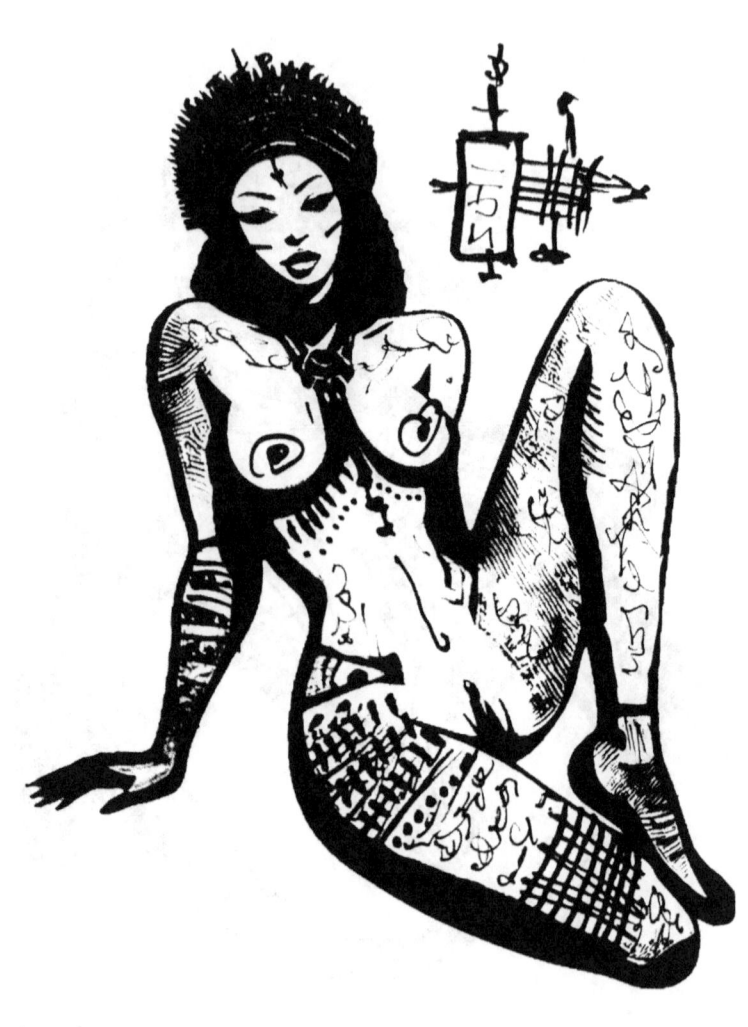

Lee. Acrylic Ink Marker on paper. 2022

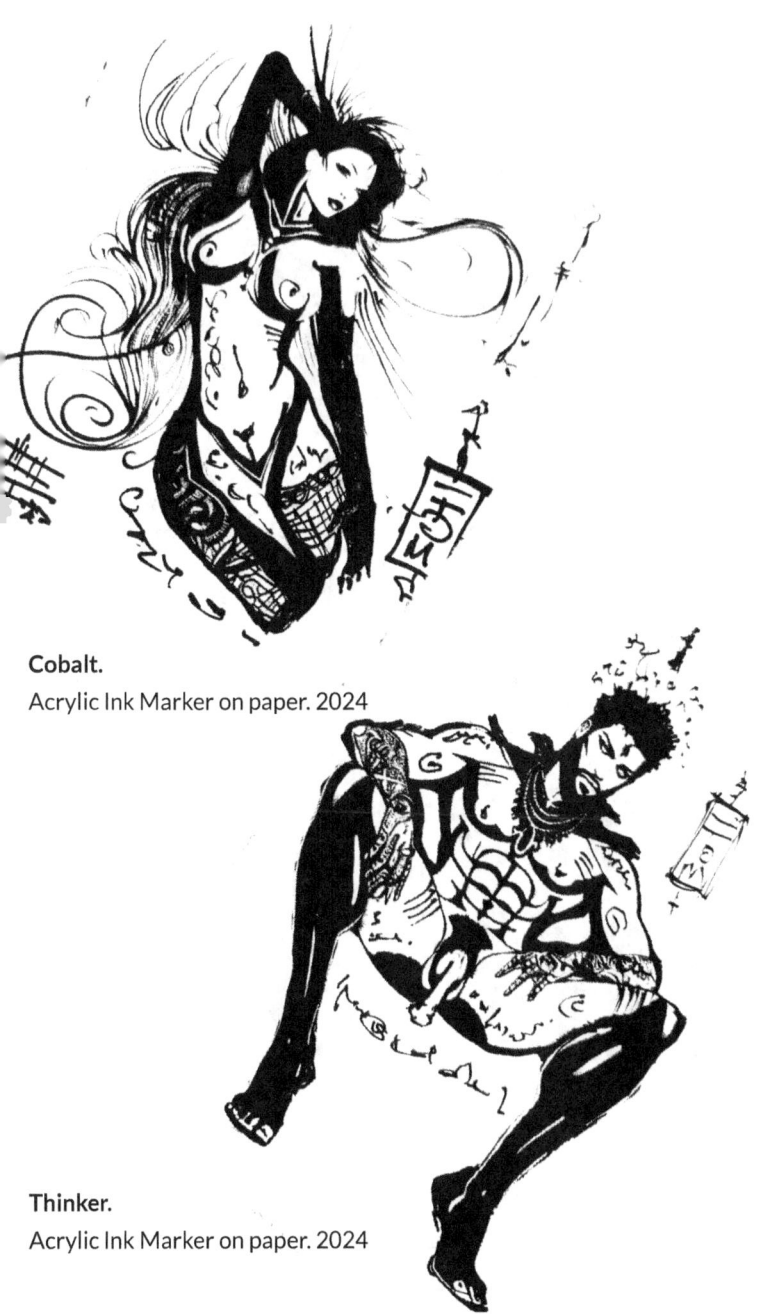

Cobalt.
Acrylic Ink Marker on paper. 2024

Thinker.
Acrylic Ink Marker on paper. 2024

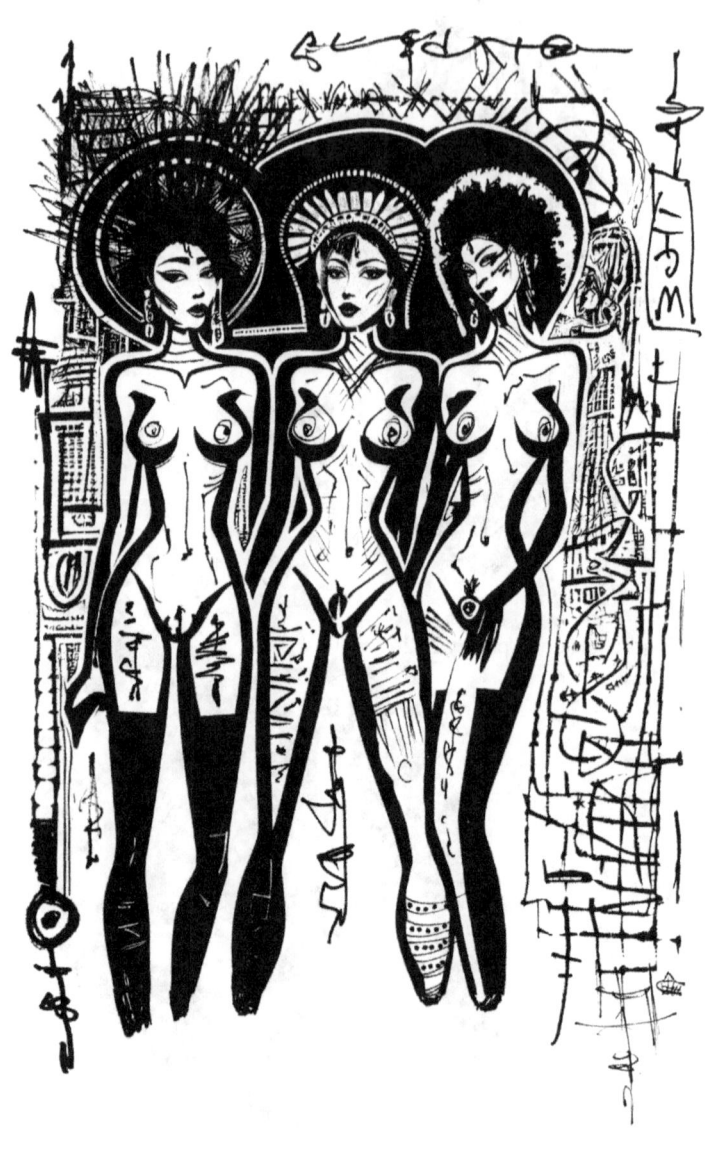

Shopping. Acrylic Ink Marker on paper. 2024

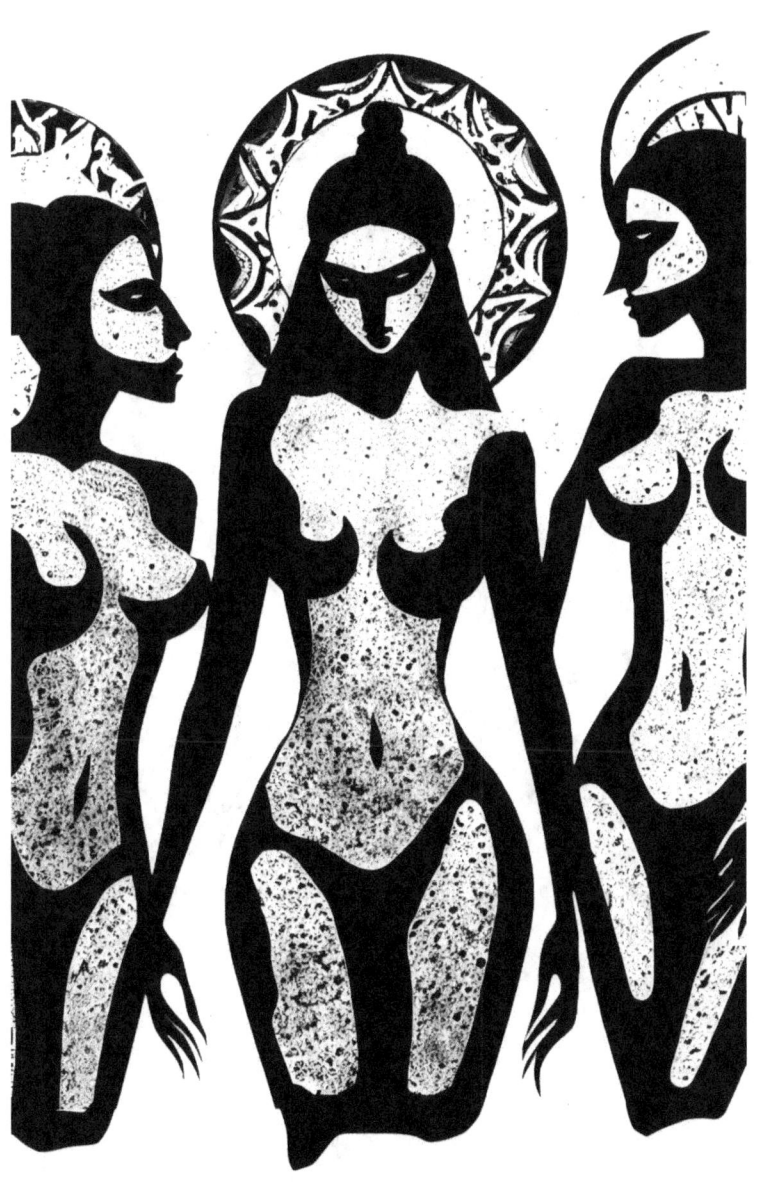

Church of Three. Acrylic Ink Marker on paper. 2020

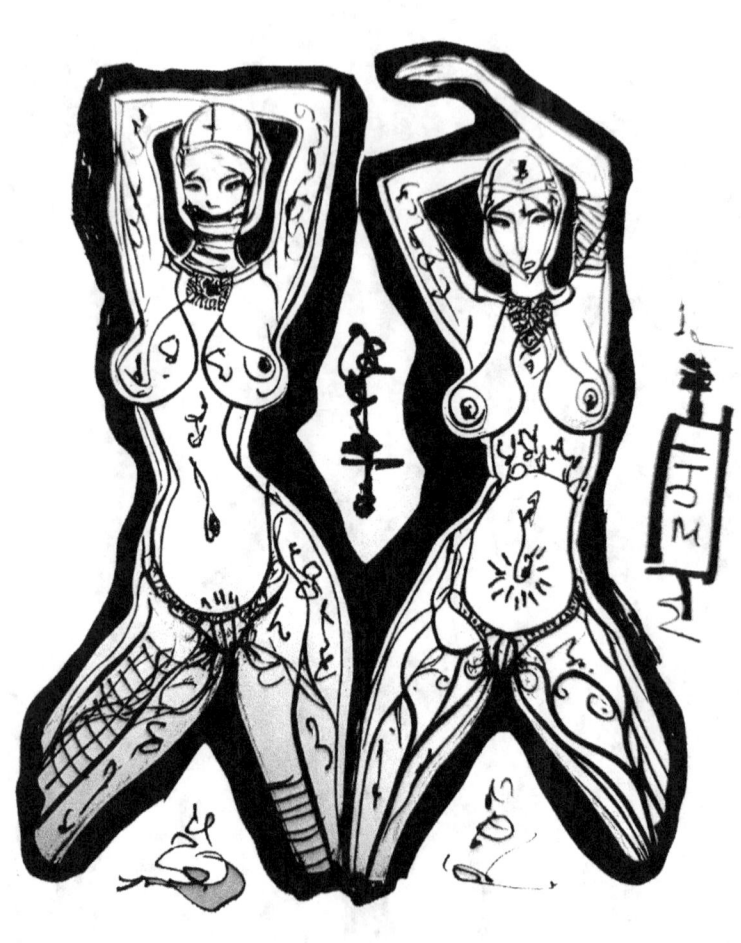

Skin Gods.   Acrylic Ink Marker on paper. 2020

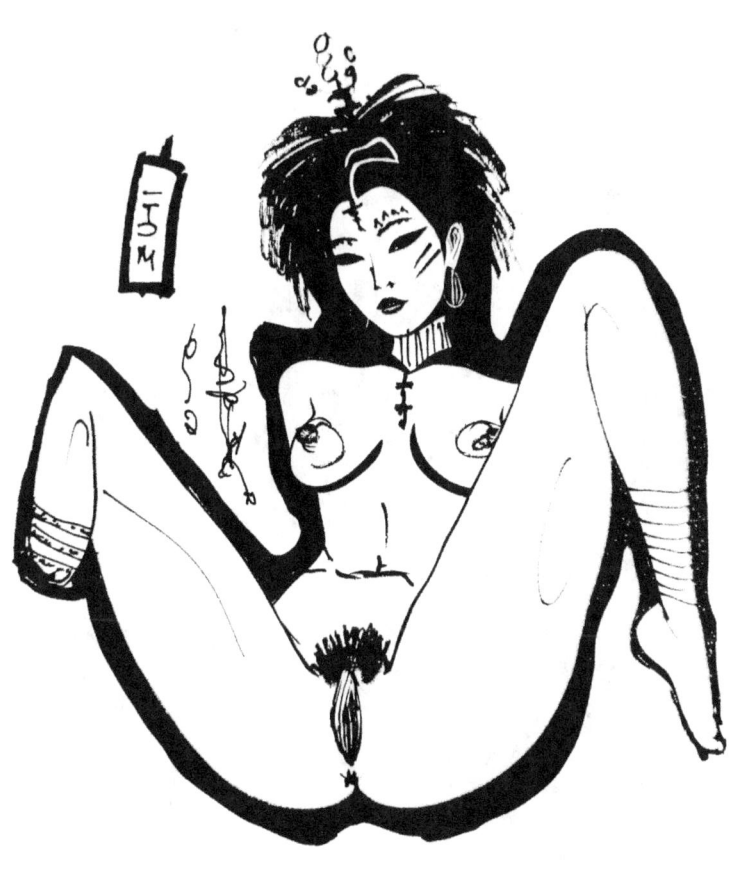

Sun. Acrylic Ink Marker on paper. 2024

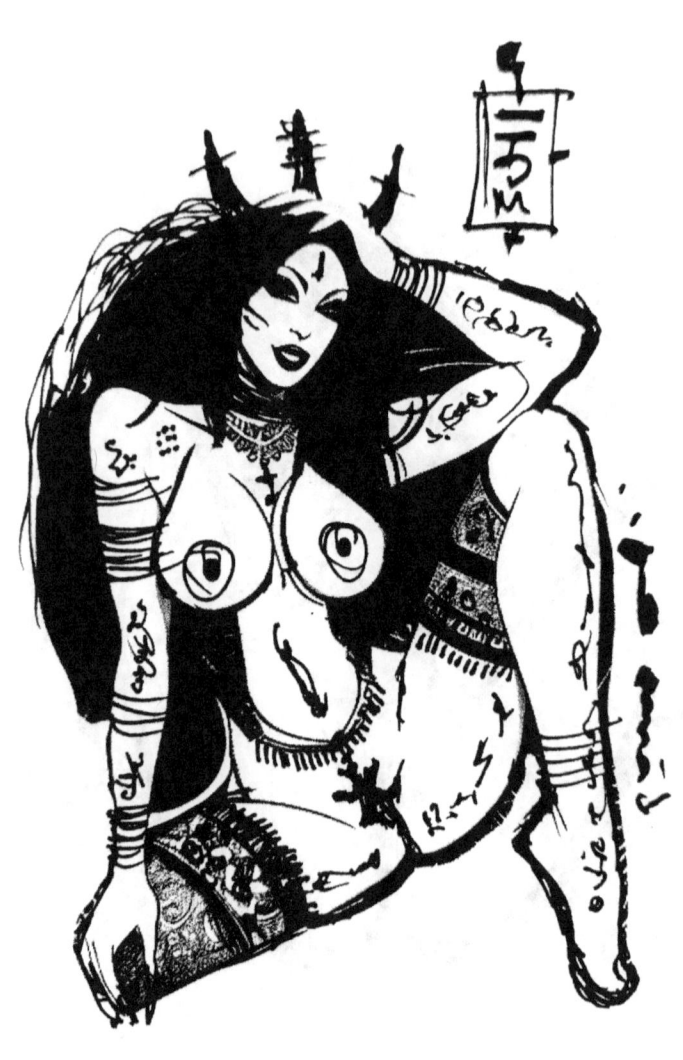

Jessica. Acrylic Ink Marker on paper. 2024

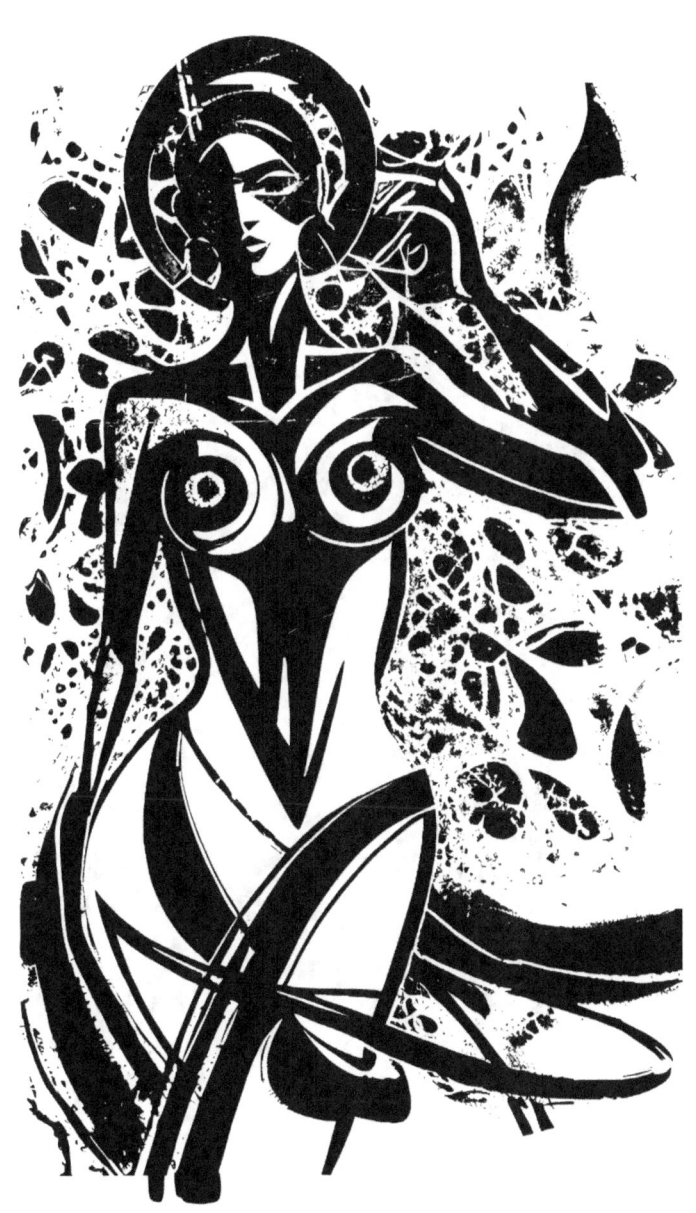

Eternity. Acrylic Ink Marker on paper. 2024

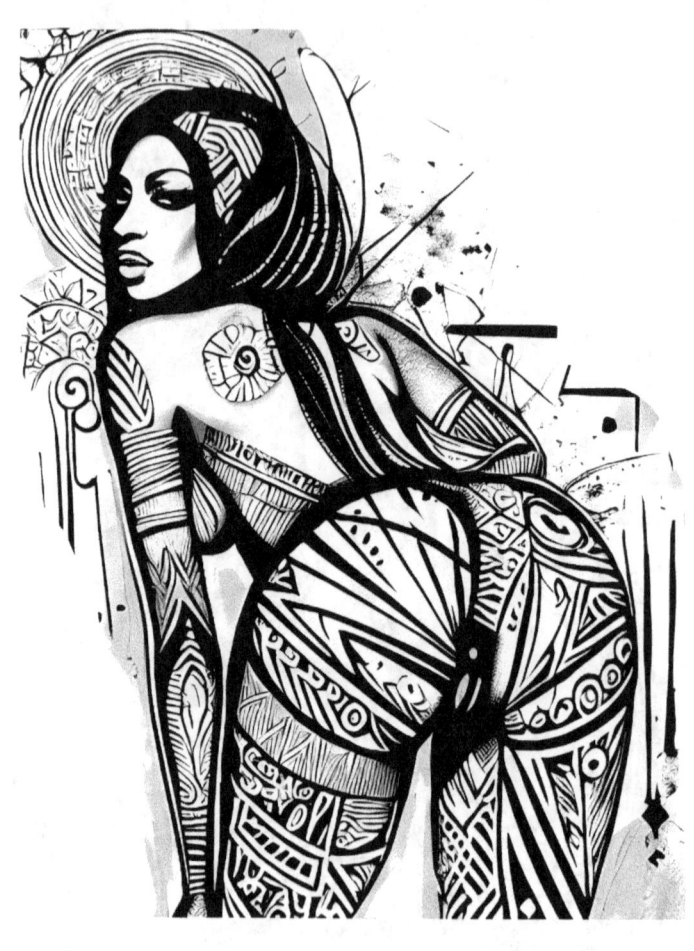

Coachella Girl. Acrylic Ink Marker on paper. 2020

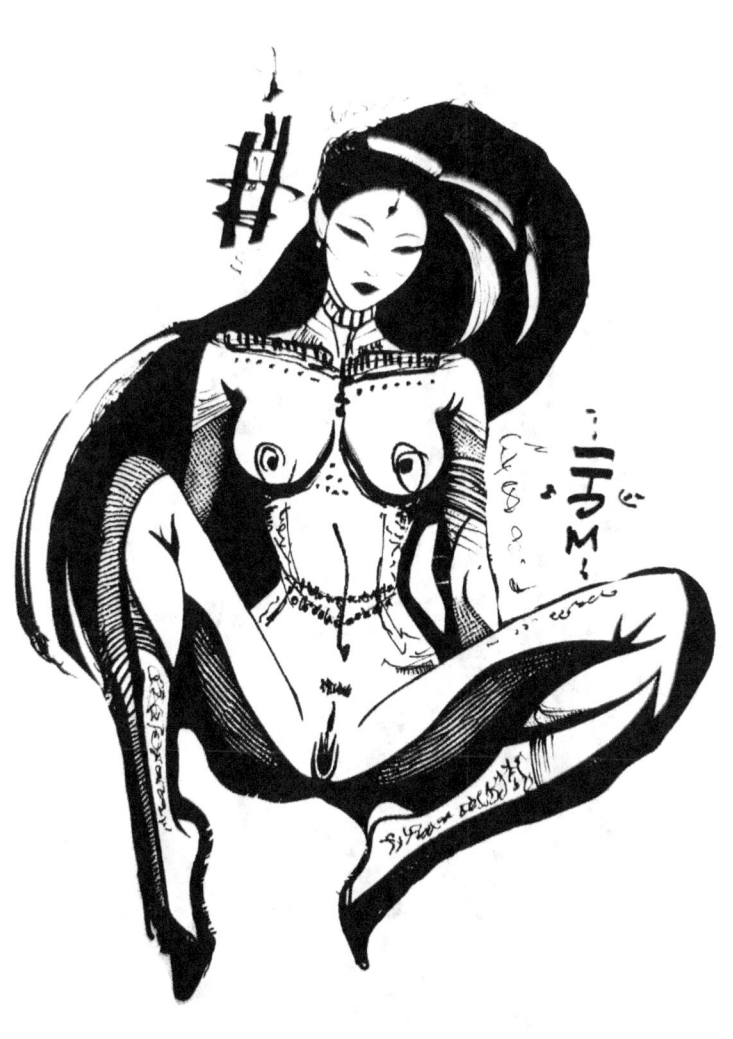

Spider. Acrylic Ink Marker on paper. 2023

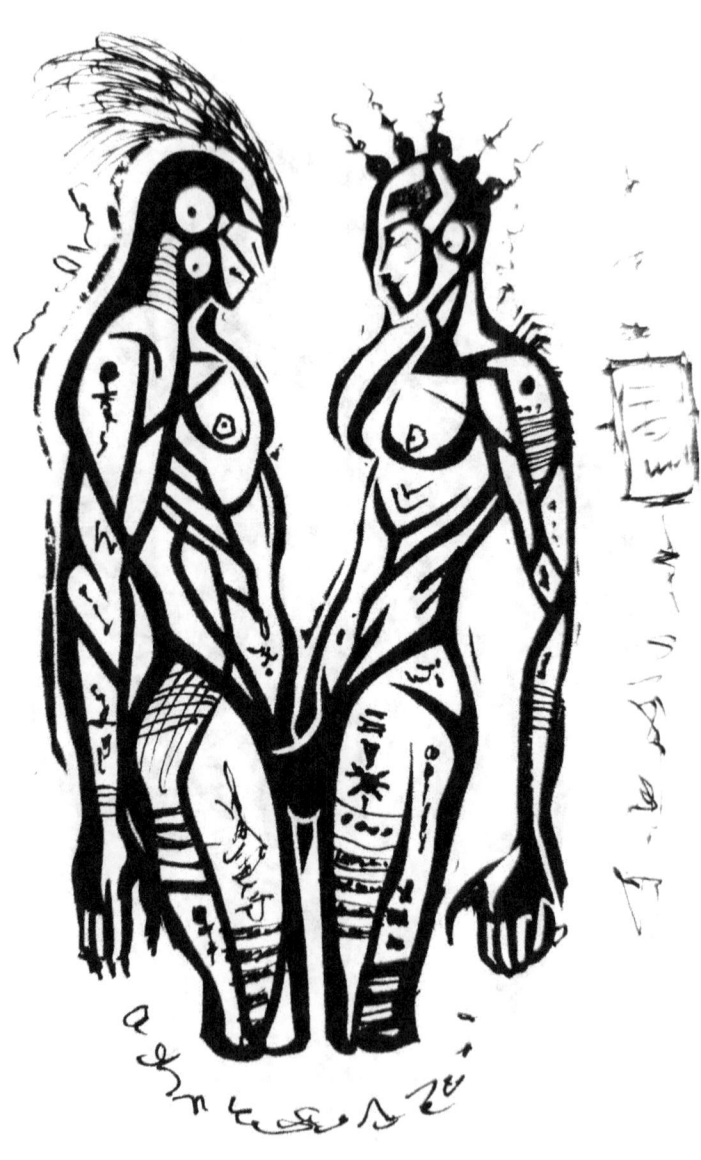

Robot Twins. Acrylic Ink Marker on paper. 2020

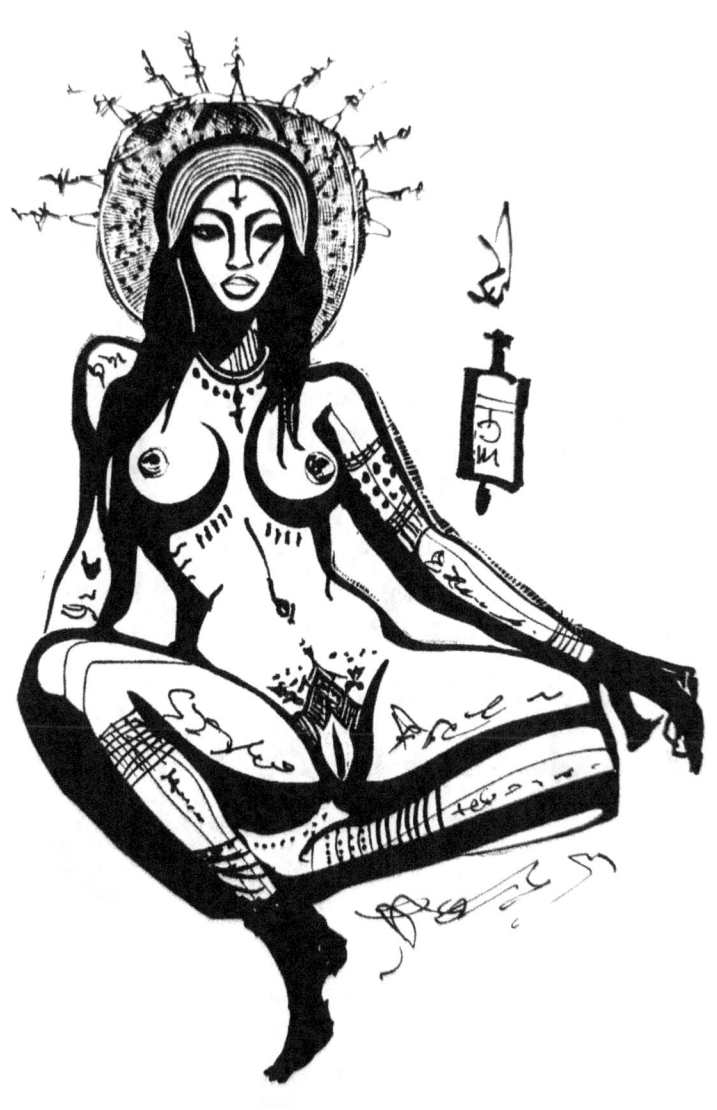

Alana. Acrylic Ink Marker on paper. 2021

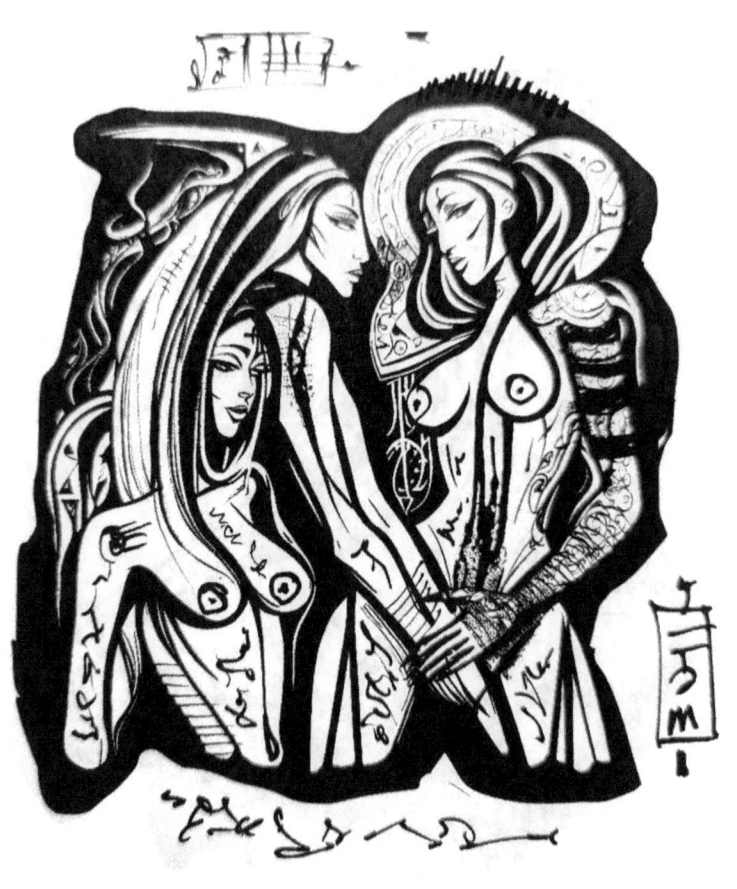

Eleganza. Acrylic Ink Marker on paper. 2024

Where in the World

One of the things I tried really hard to do during this entire show was to create a sense of "sacred sexuality, a sort of religious fervor and presentiment in charaters but without a specific religion or culture.

If you aren't sure what that means, don't worry, I'm not, either. I think there are ways to make something feel like it has religious import. headdresses, bands, robes, braided sashes, ostentatious displays, etc.

The problem is that these things are usuually in color. But if you break down some of the earliest displays of reverence you can see a sort of symbolic chain connecting them all, from cave paintings to hieroglyphs to stained glass and woodcuts. There is a kind of flat intentionality to it all, a sort of cultural idolotry built from the simplest forms into more complex sort of engrams,

Rosaries, for example, are simple beads, simple chain, a simple cross shape, put together and then hyperstylized in the areas in between. This expresses a "religion" in a way.

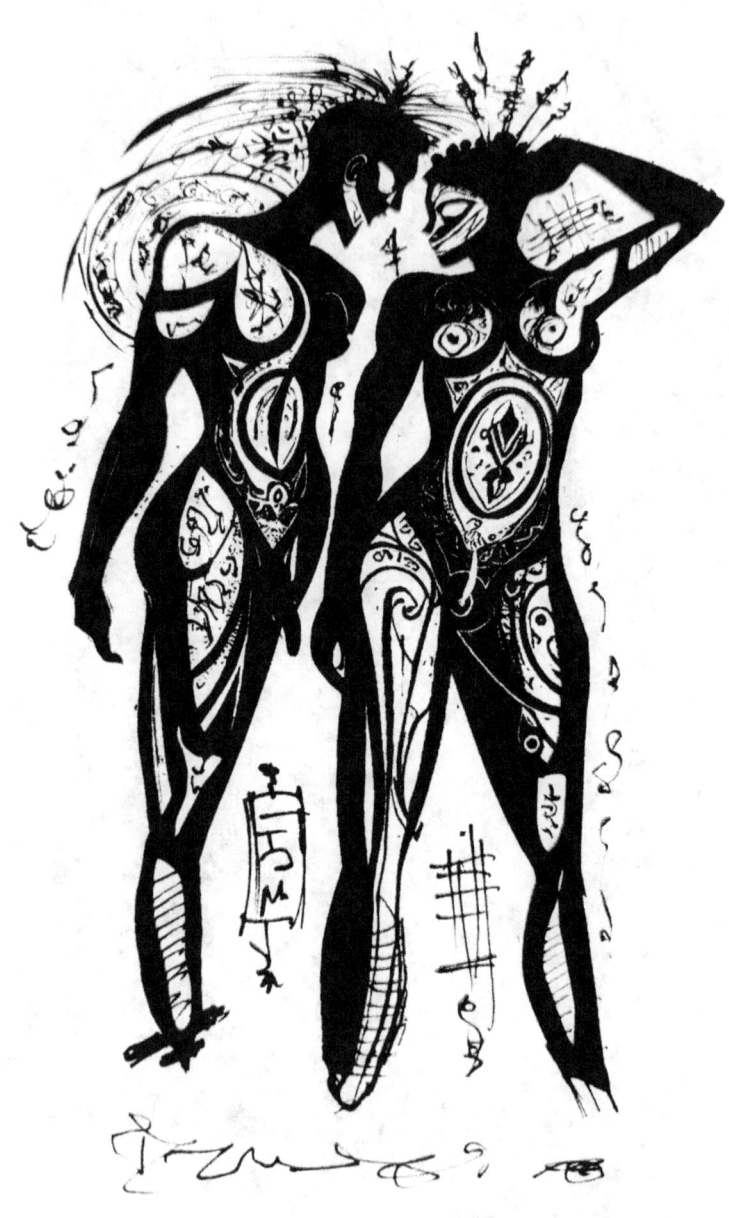

Converge. Acrylic Ink Marker on paper. 2024

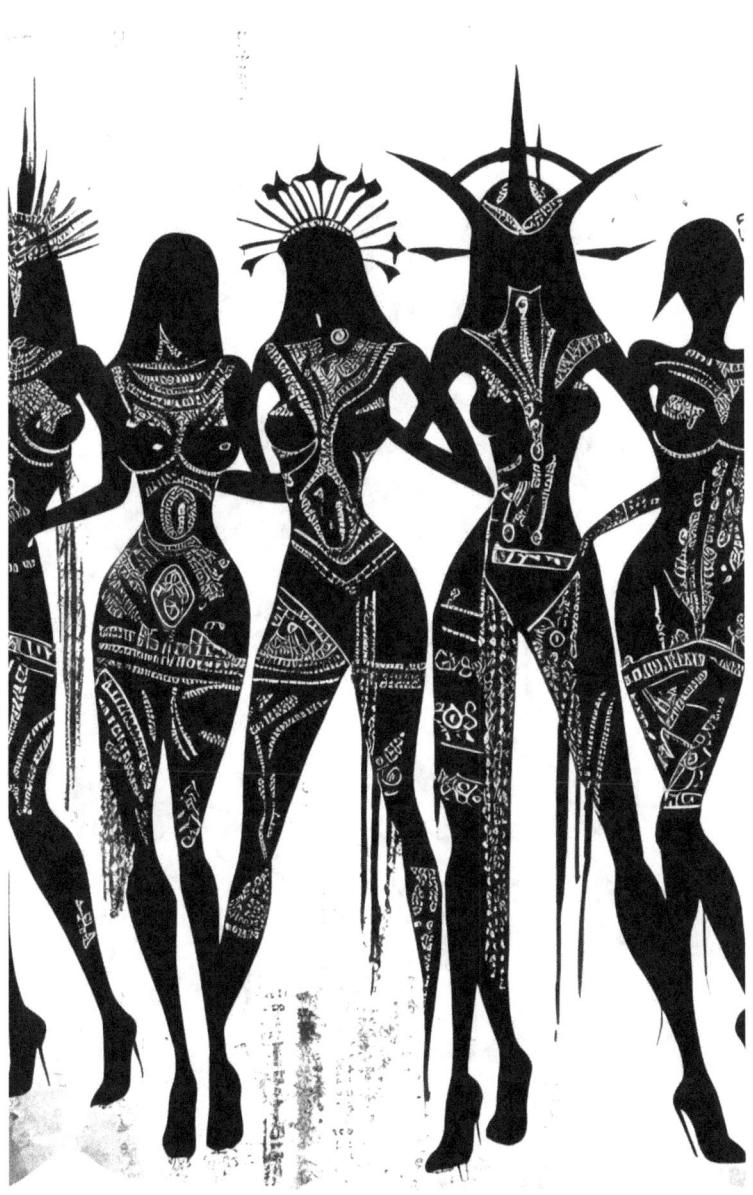

Flats. Acrylic Ink Marker on paper
(digitally scanned and inverted and then drawn in again). 2022

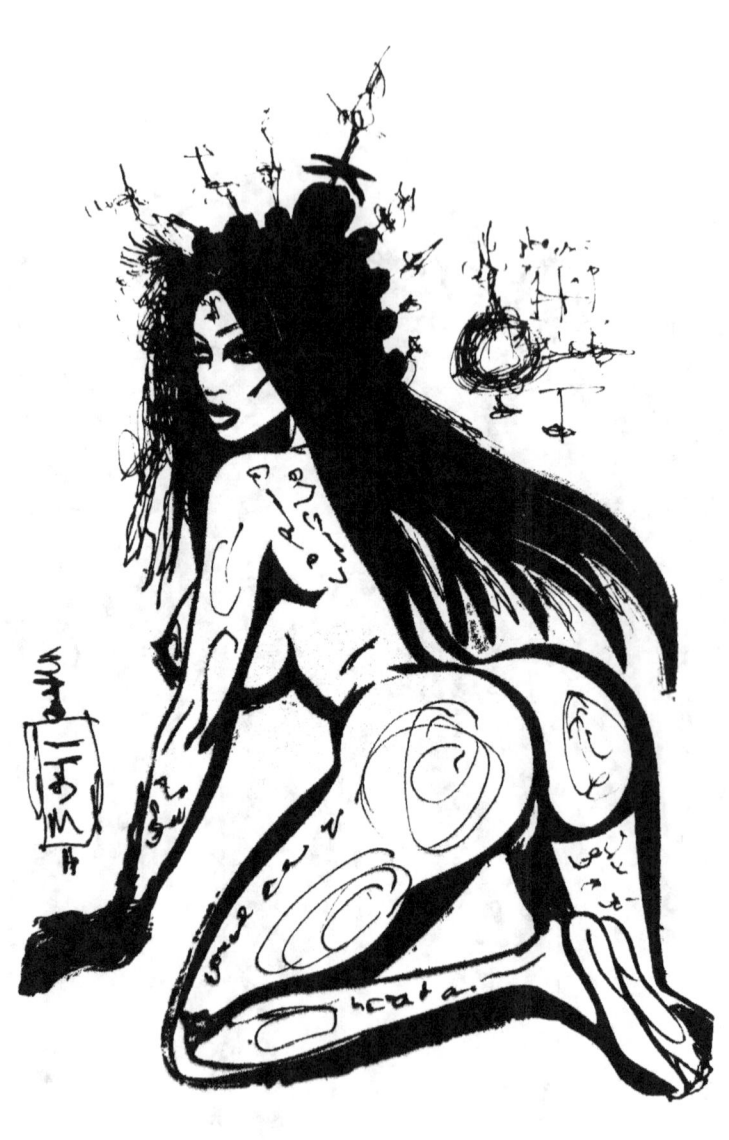

Canta. Acrylic Ink Marker on paper. 2024

Hina
Acrylic Ink Marker on paper. 2023

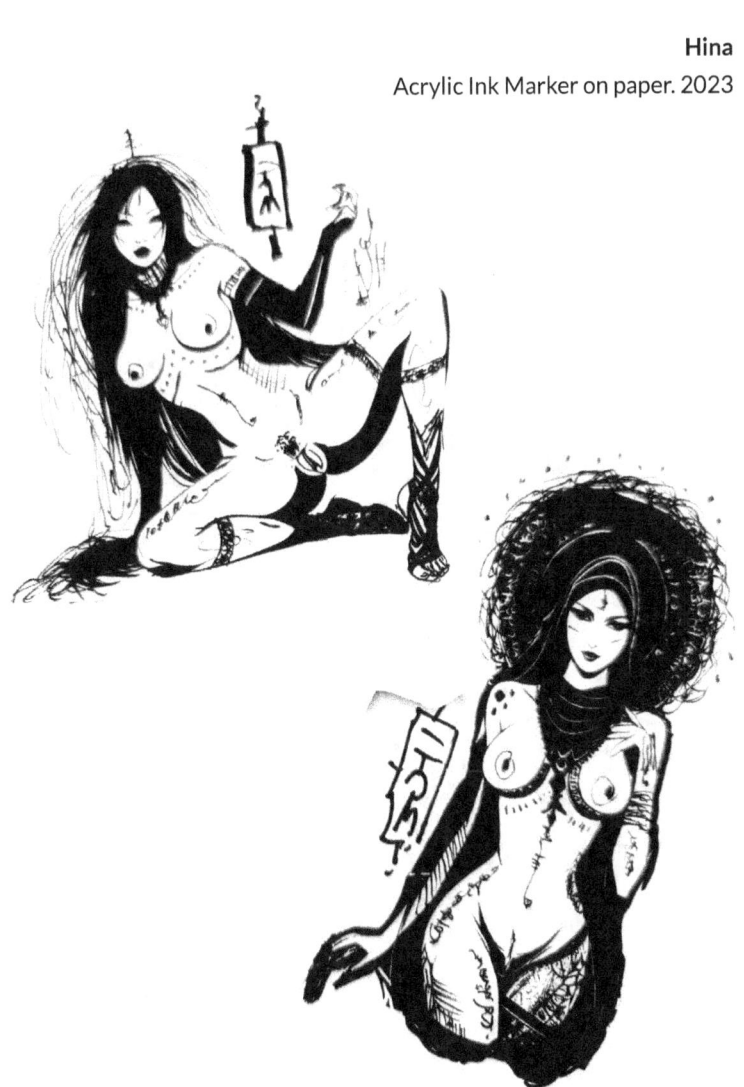

Meg
Acrylic Ink Marker on paper. 2023

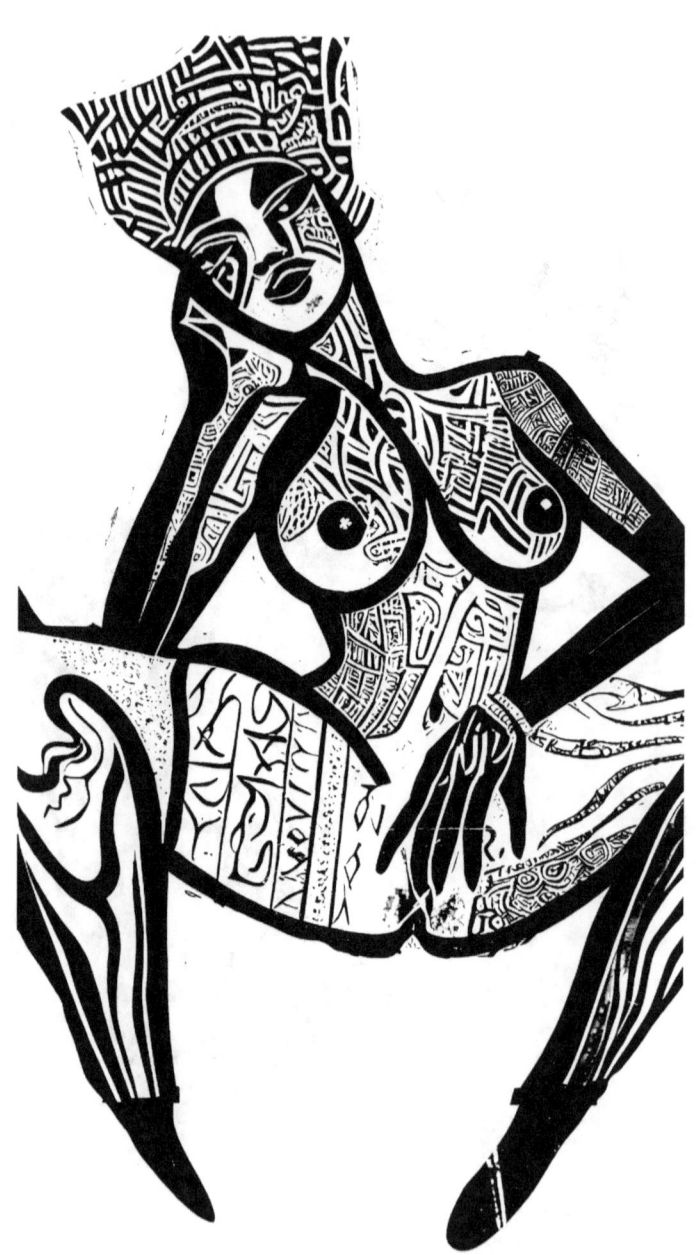

The Wild Sister. Acrylic Ink Marker on paper. 2020

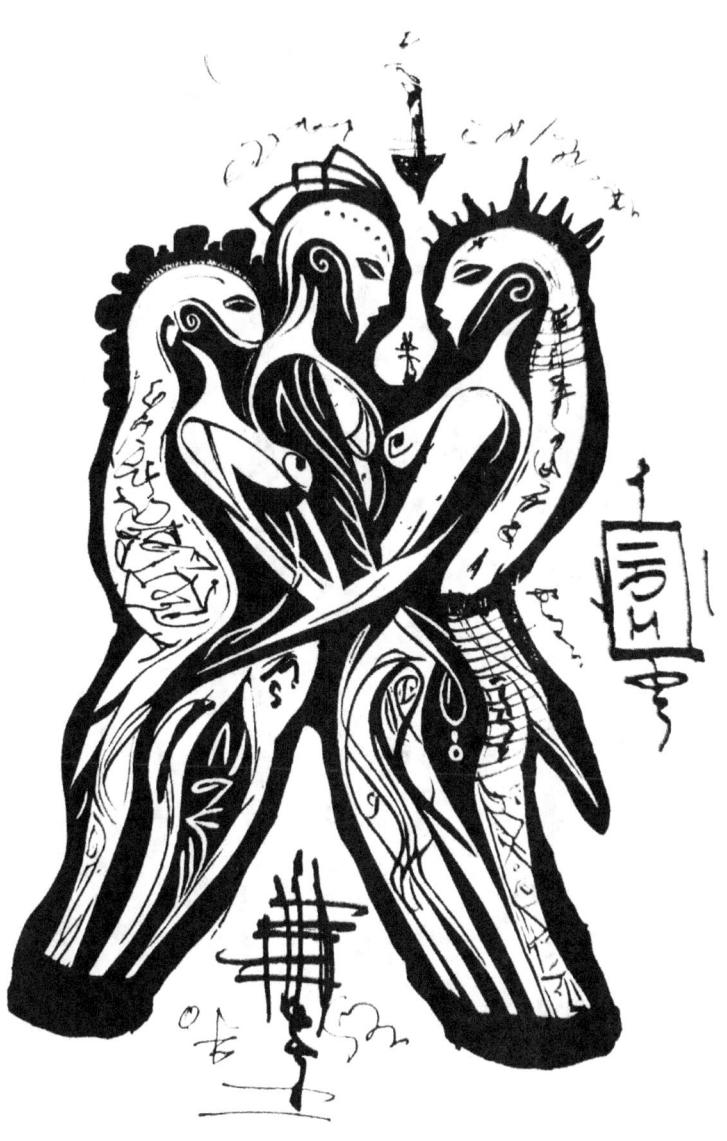

Alliance. Acrylic Ink Marker on paper. 2024

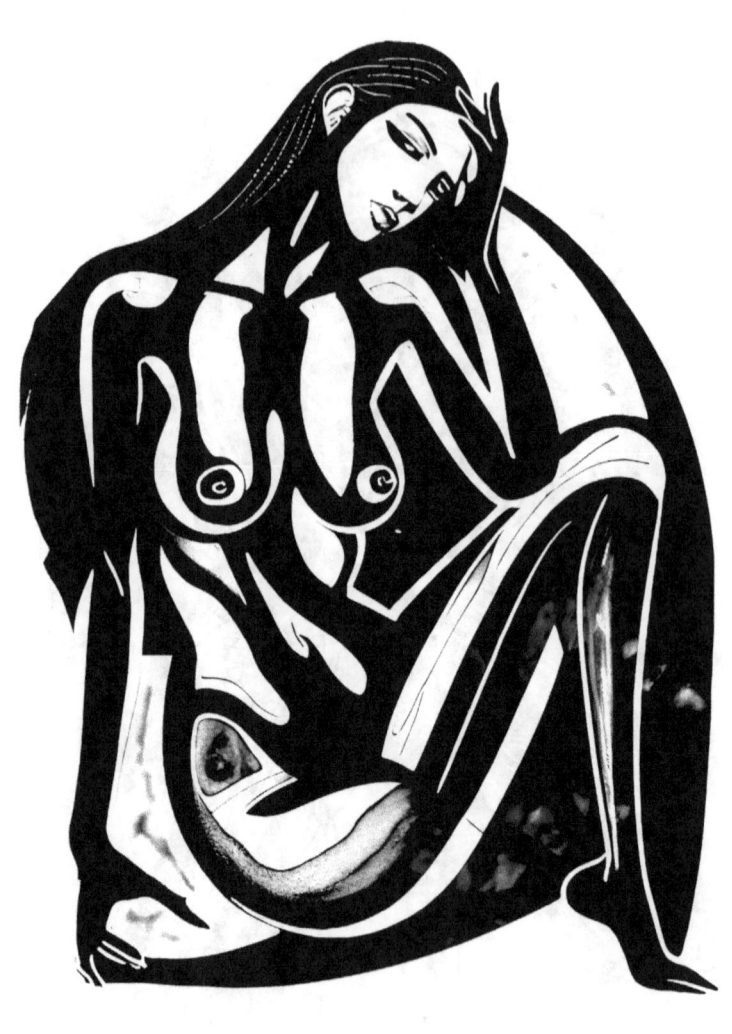

The Other Sister. Acrylic Ink Marker on paper.
(With water) 2020

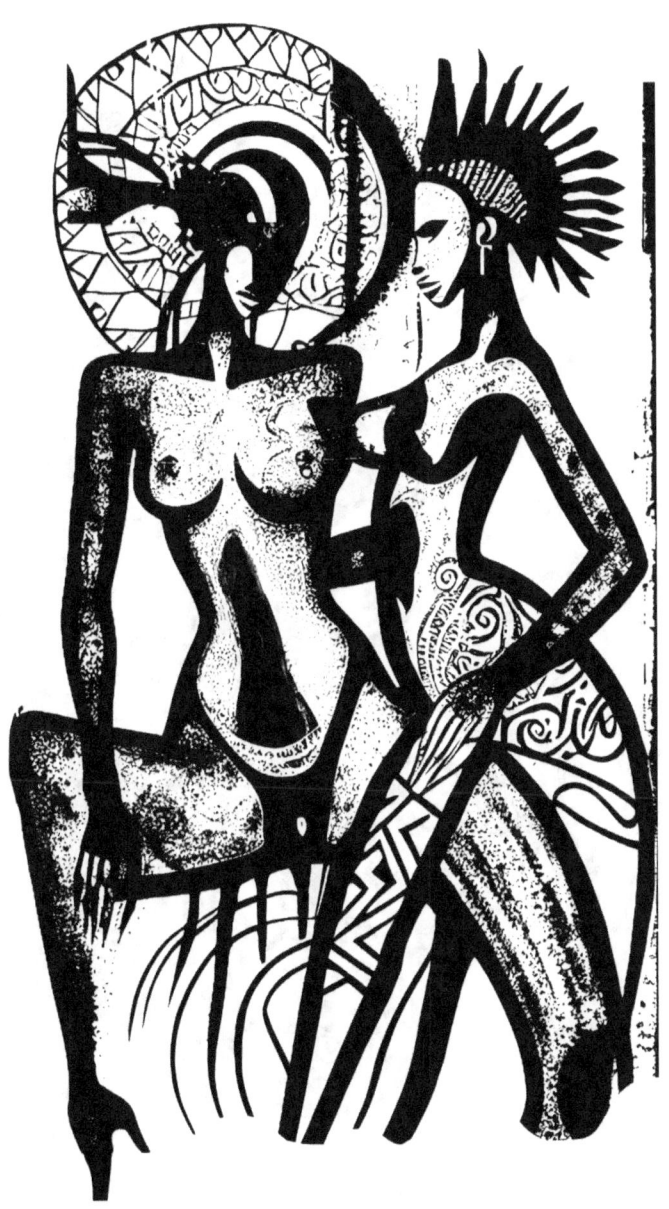

Elated. Acrylic Ink Marker on paper with texture ruubbing. 2021

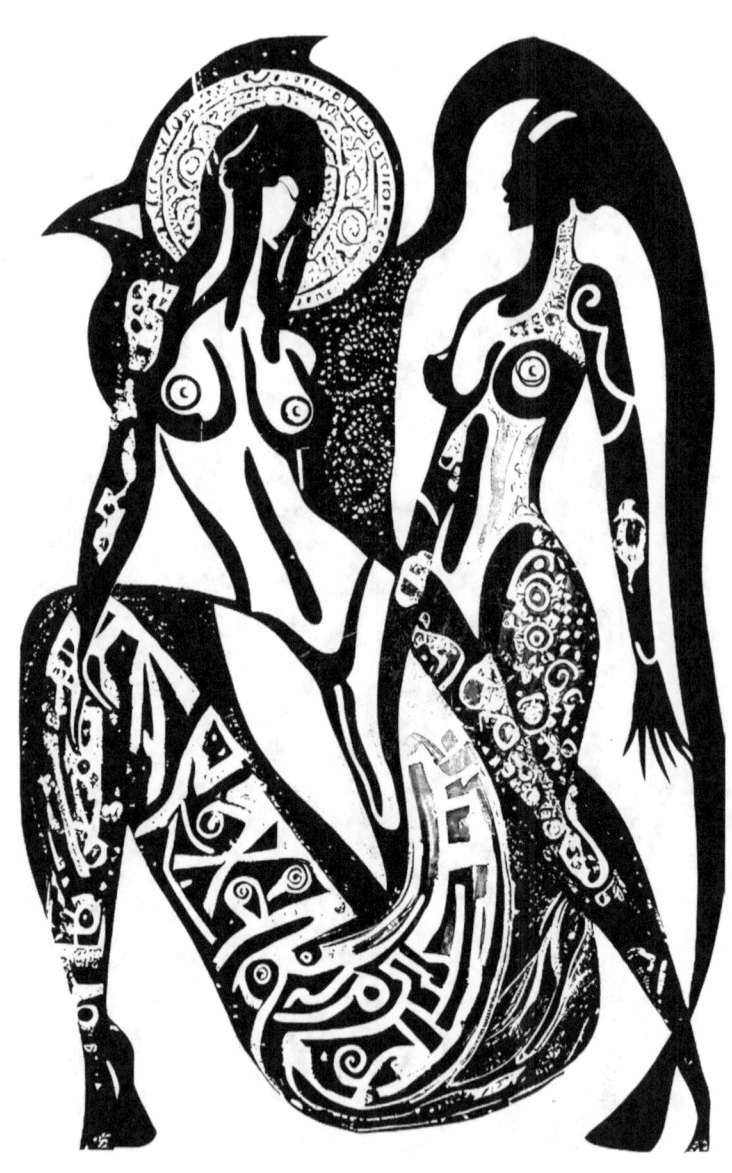

Infinity Dress. Acrylic Ink Marker on paper.
(Ink Rubbing on texturea) 2020

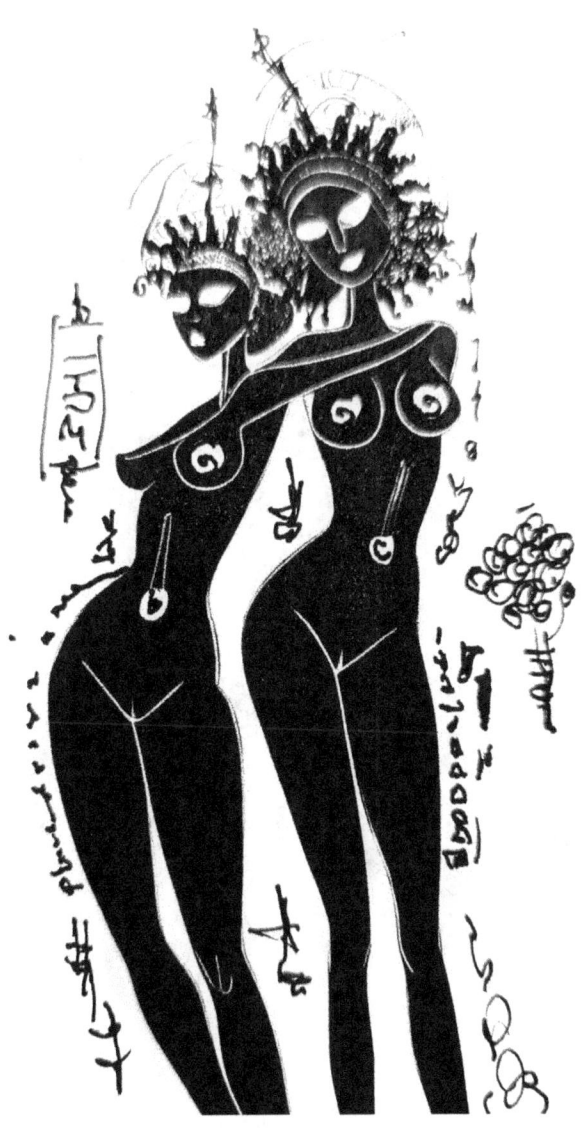

Loved. Acrylic Ink Marker on paper with texture ruubbing. 2024

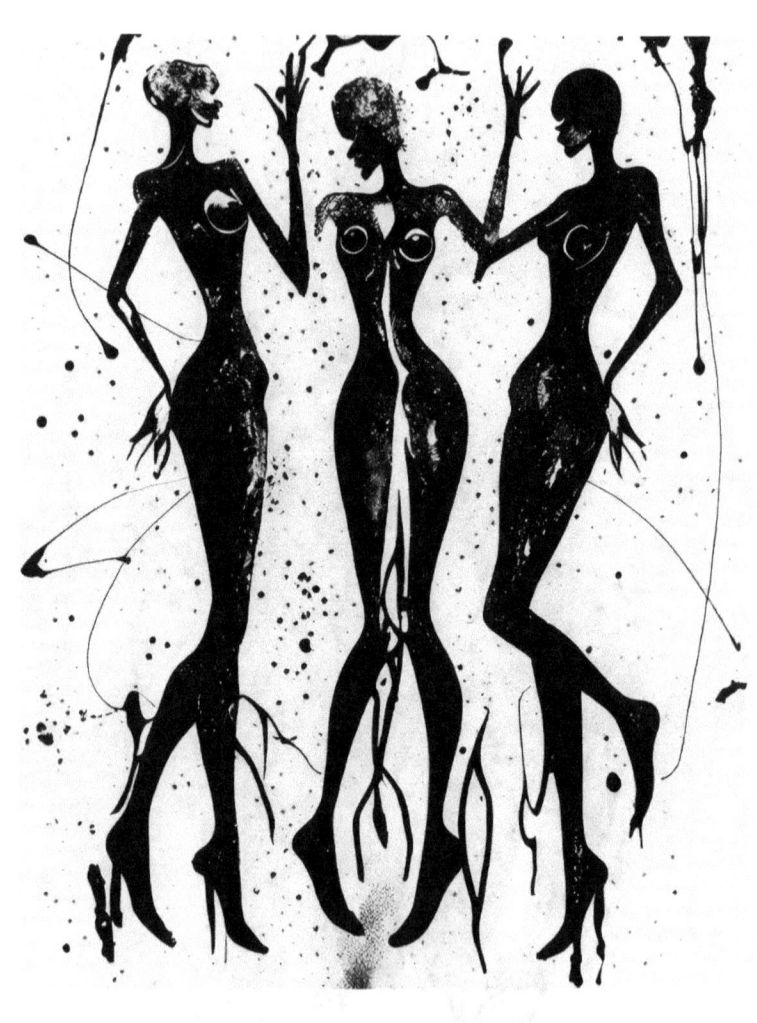

Infinity Dress. Acrylic Ink Marker on paper.
(with paint splatters) 2020

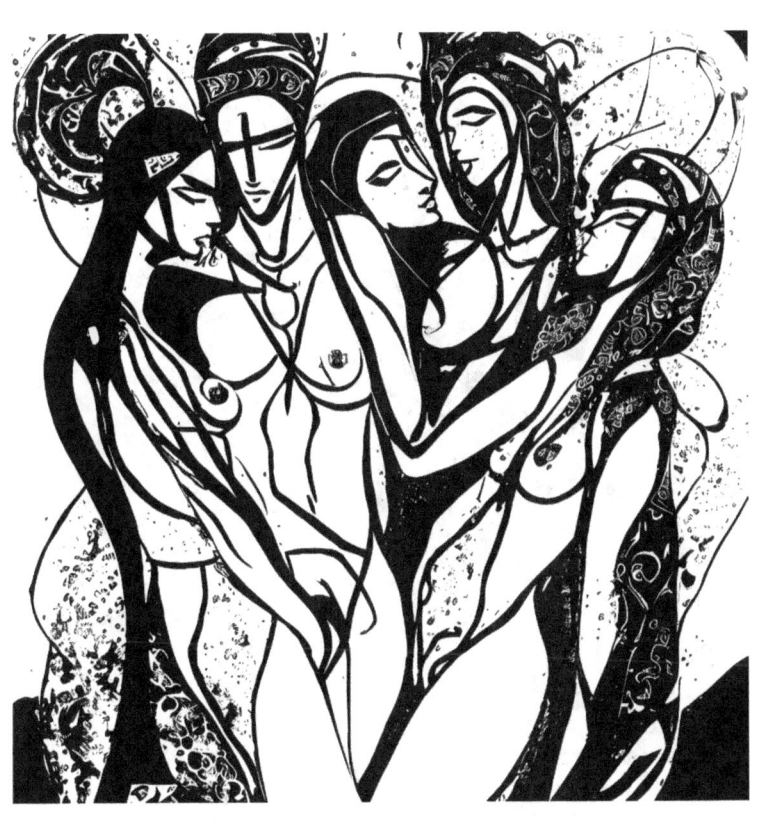

Family. Acrylic Ink Marker on paper with texture rubbing.
(blown up and painted for show.) 2022

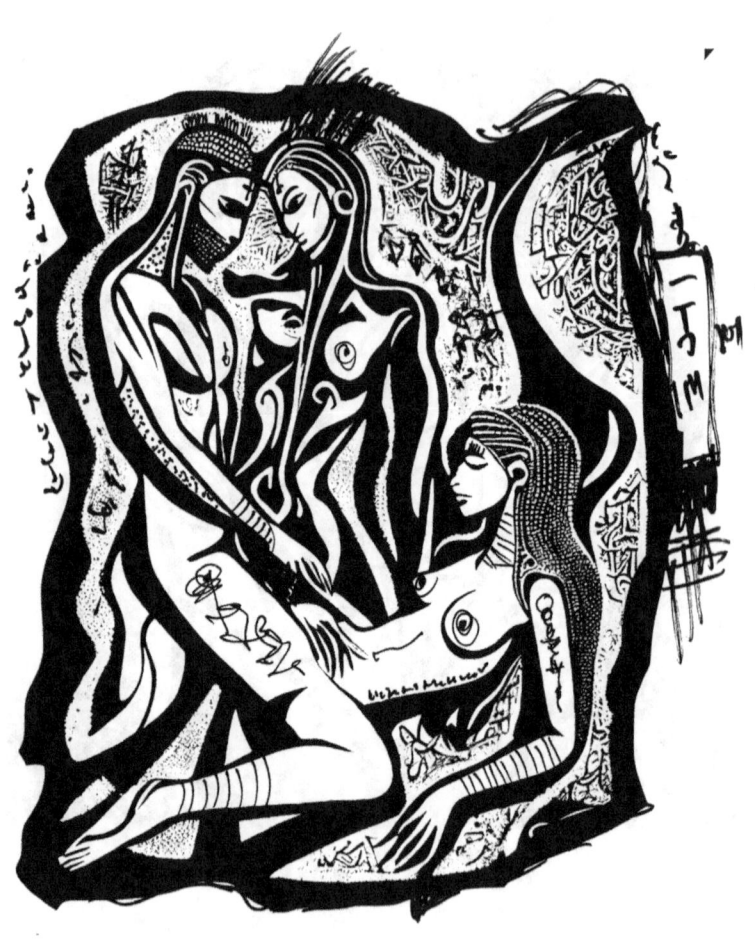

Playing Robot. Acrylic Ink Marker on paper.
(Texture rubbing) 2022

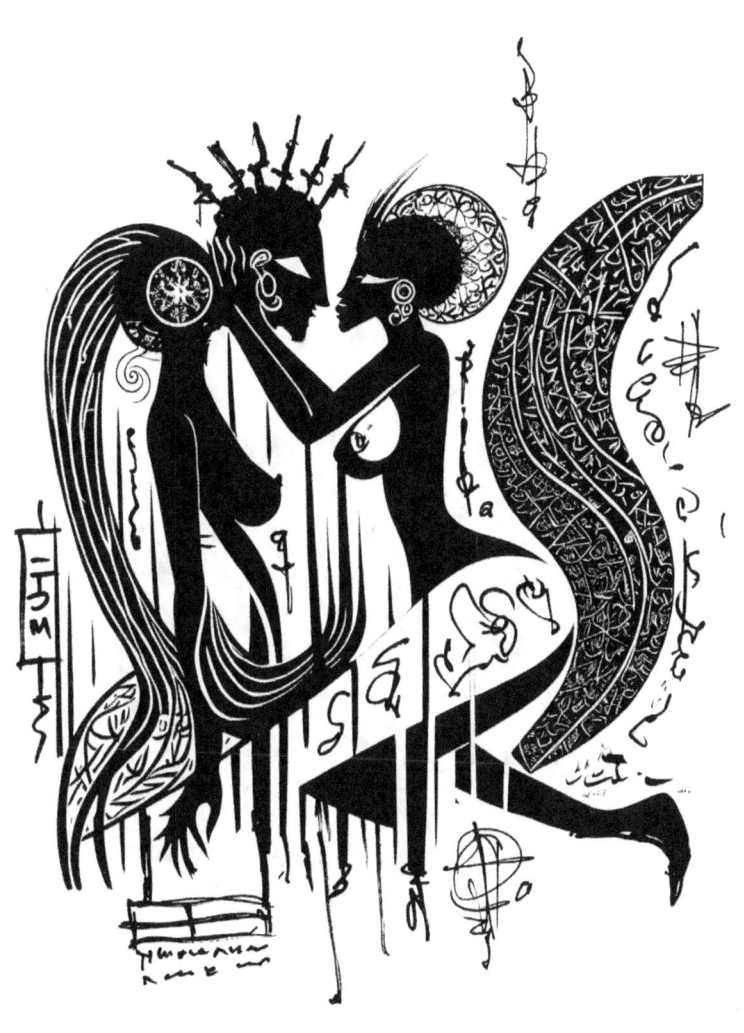

Give Me Head. Acrylic Ink Marker on paper with texture rubbing.
(Digital inversion and redraw) 2023

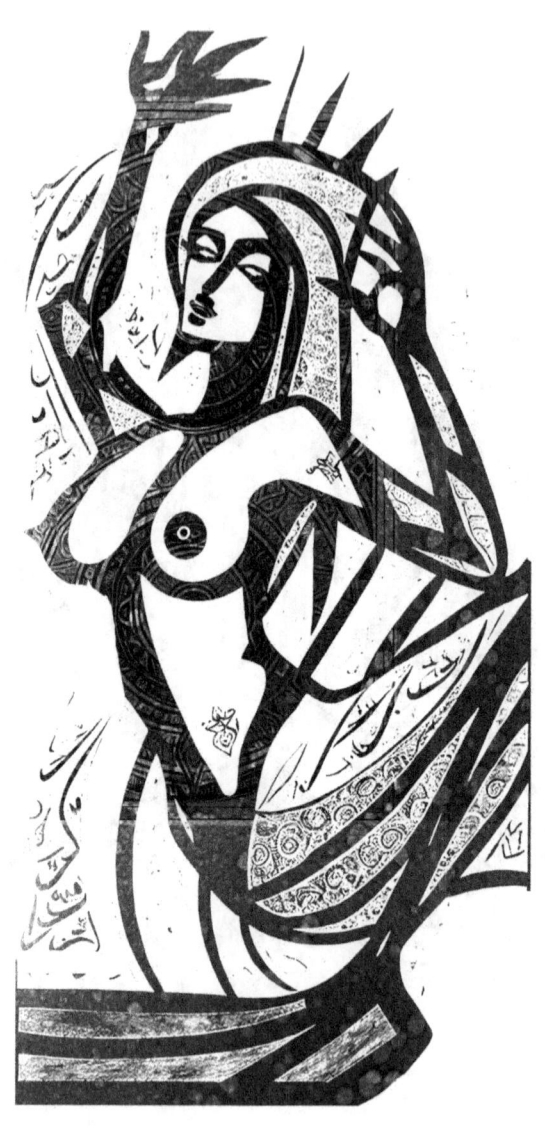

Serenaded / Snake Dance. Acrylic Ink Marker on paper.
(Texture rubbing) 2017

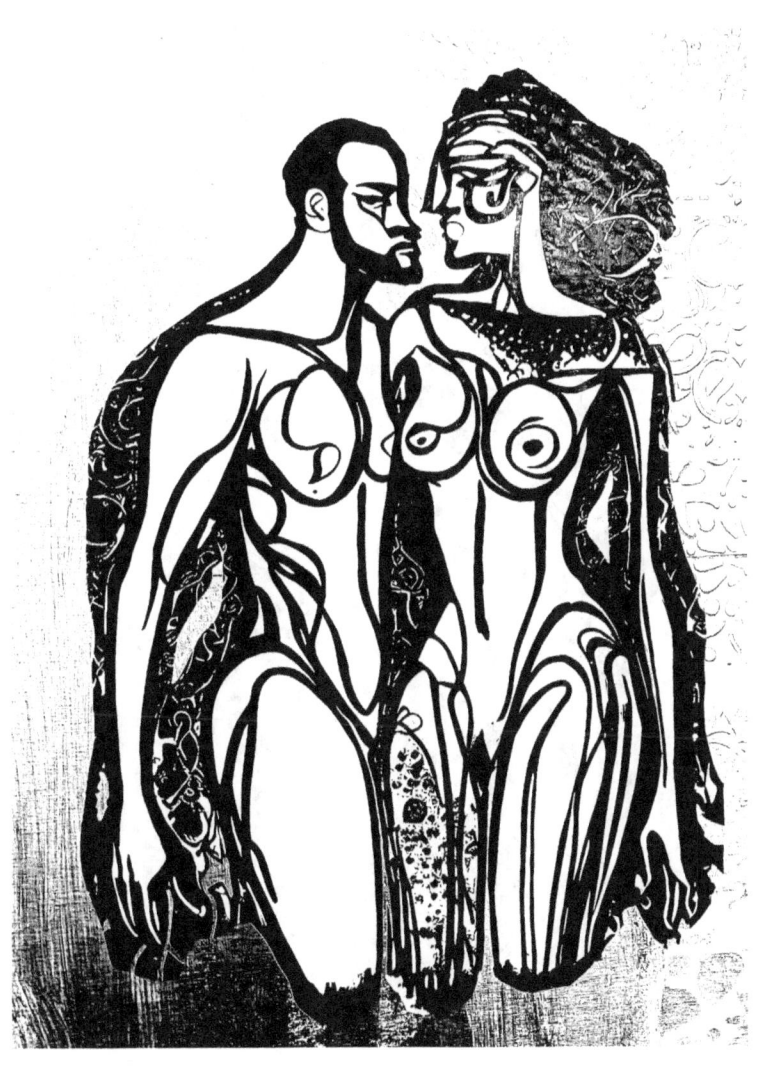

Apollo and Athena. Acrylic Ink Marker on paper with texture rubbing. 2016 (the oldest one here)

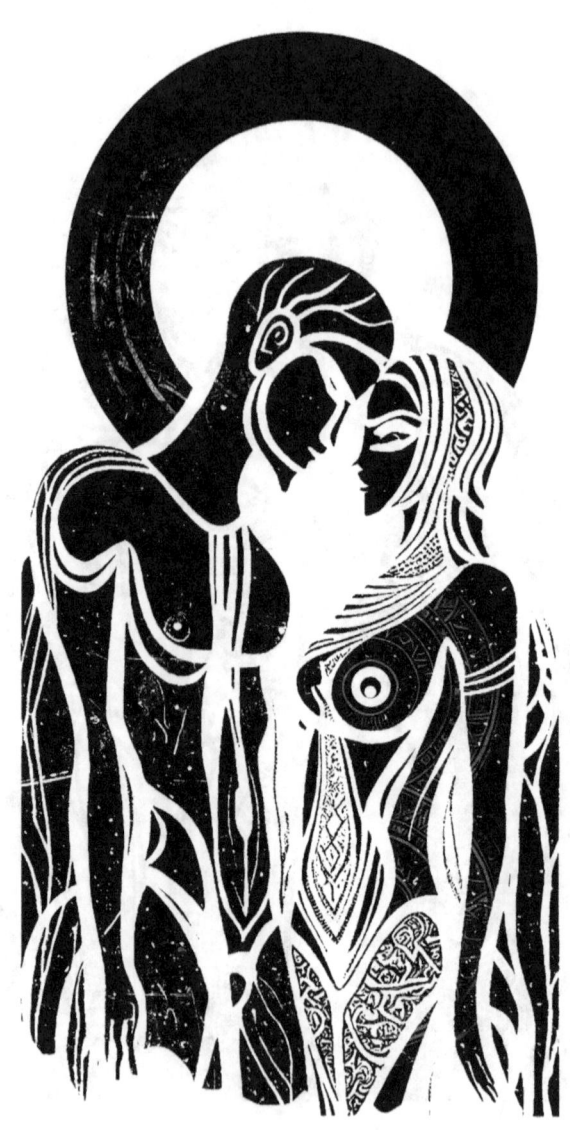

Lovedolls. Acrylic Ink Marker on paper.
(Texture rubbing) 2018

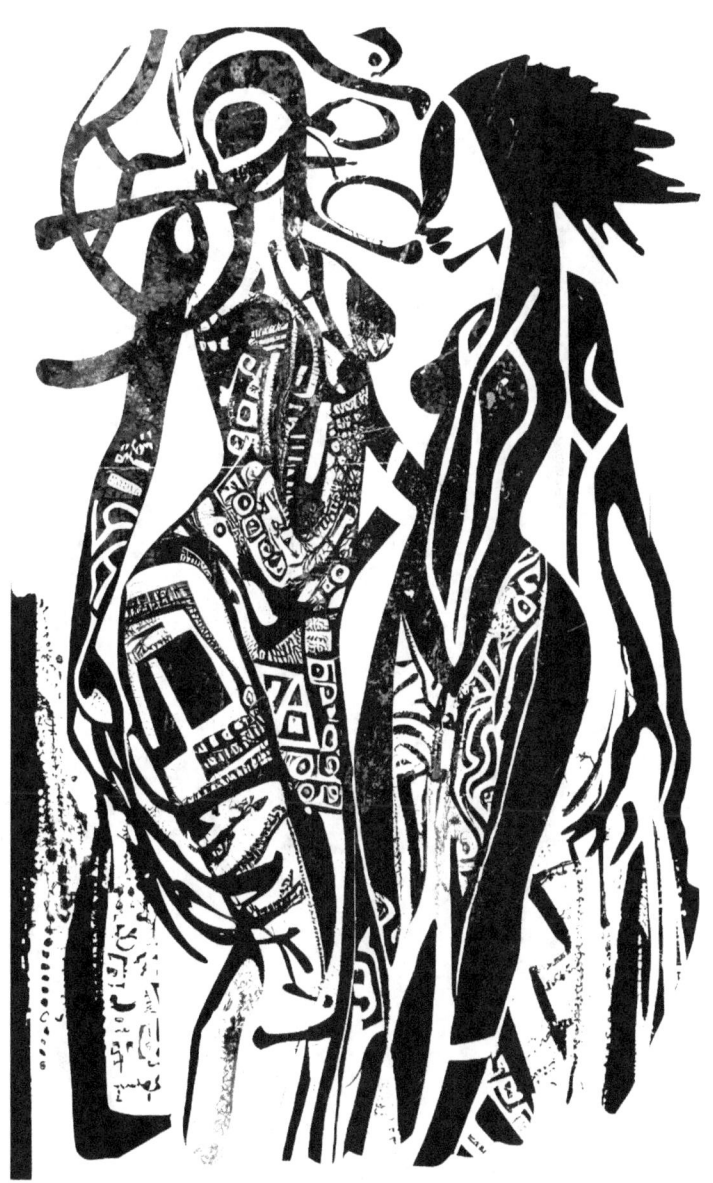

Brand Theater Acrylic Ink Marker on paper with texture rubbing.
2018

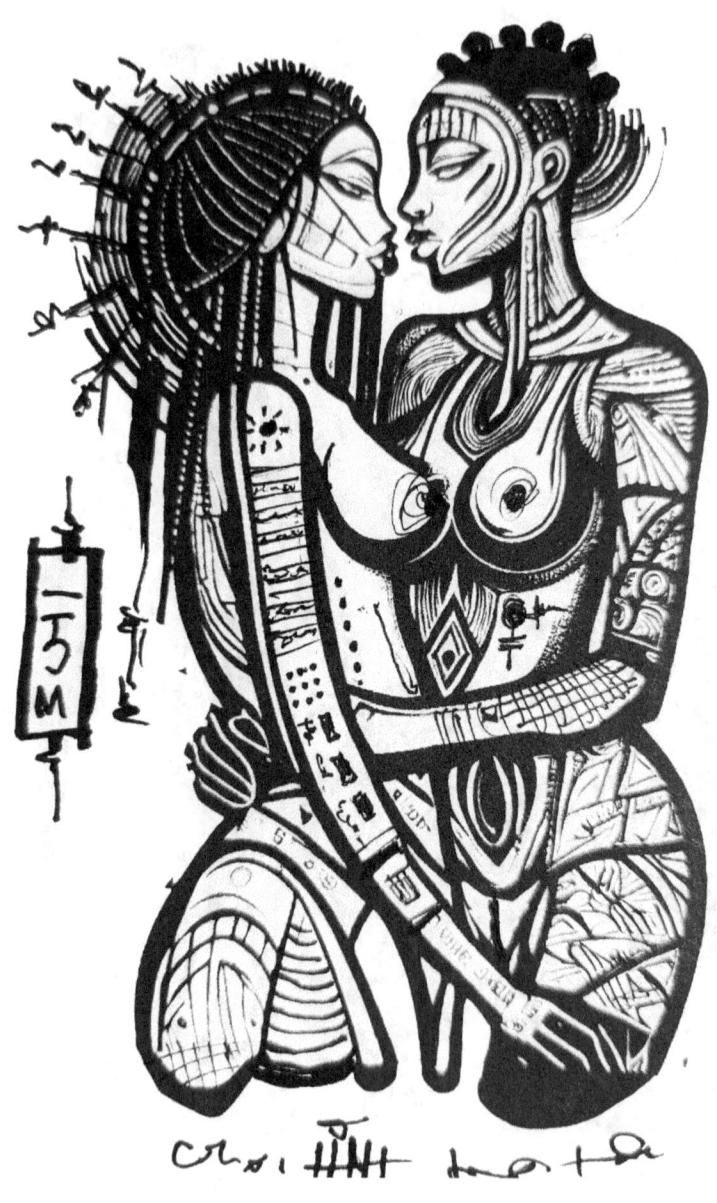

Senegali. Acrylic Ink Marker on paper. 2024

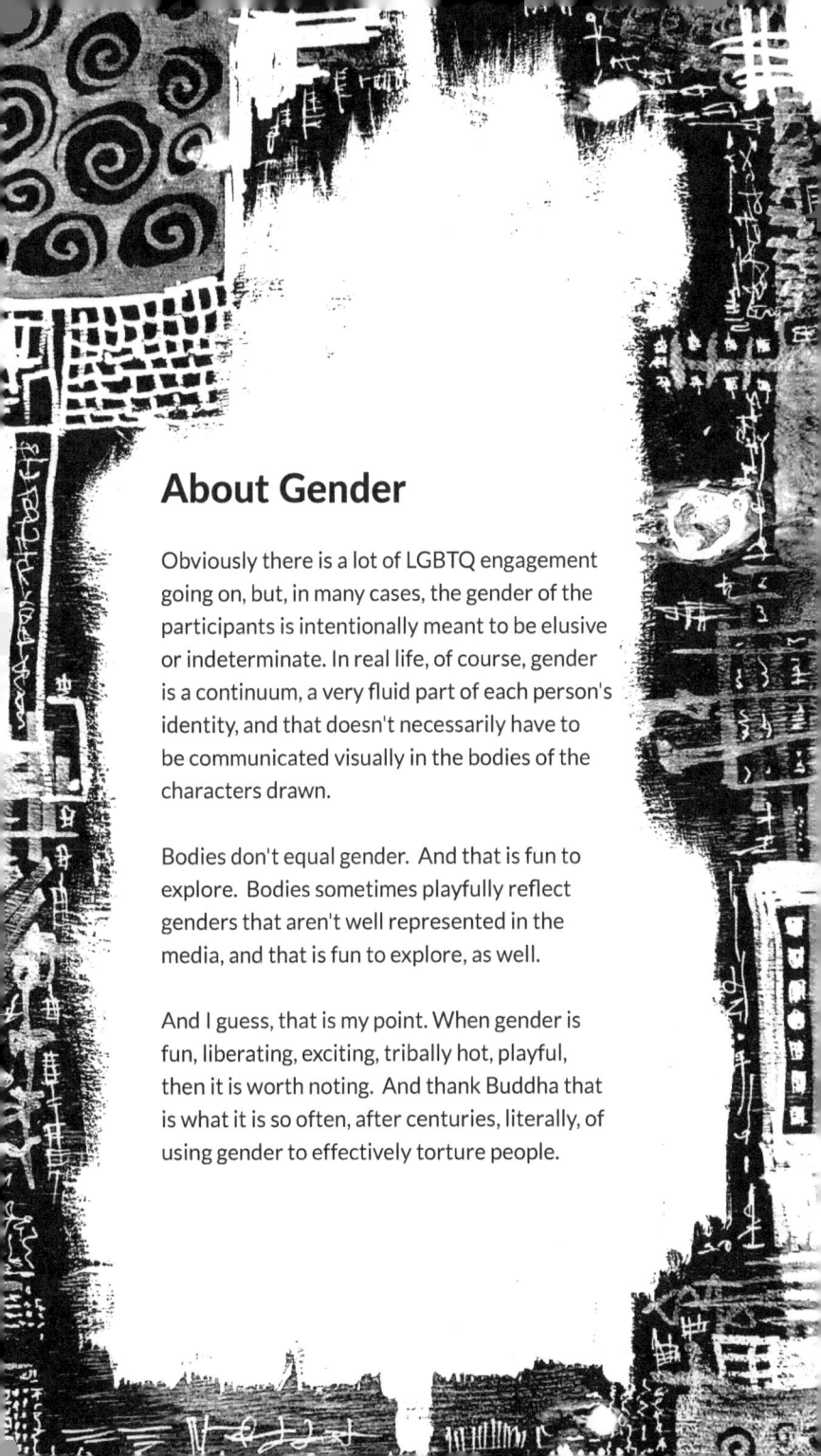

About Gender

Obviously there is a lot of LGBTQ engagement going on, but, in many cases, the gender of the participants is intentionally meant to be elusive or indeterminate. In real life, of course, gender is a continuum, a very fluid part of each person's identity, and that doesn't necessarily have to be communicated visually in the bodies of the characters drawn.

Bodies don't equal gender. And that is fun to explore. Bodies sometimes playfully reflect genders that aren't well represented in the media, and that is fun to explore, as well.

And I guess, that is my point. When gender is fun, liberating, exciting, tribally hot, playful, then it is worth noting. And thank Buddha that is what it is so often, after centuries, literally, of using gender to effectively torture people.